NOLLYWOOD

NOLLYWOOD
The Video Phenomenon in Nigeria

Edited by
Pierre Barrot

with
Ibbo Daddy Abdoulaye
Olivier Barlet
Franck Baku Fuita
Tunde Kelani
Godefroid Bwiti Lumisa
Frédéric Noy
Don Pedro Obaseki
Tunde Oladunjoye
Ogova Ondego

Translations by
Lynn Taylor

James Currey
OXFORD

HEBN
IBADAN

Indiana University Press
BLOOMINGTON & INDIANAPOLIS

First published in English in 2008 in the United Kingdom by
James Currey
73 Botley Road
Oxford OX2 0BS
www.jamescurrey.co.uk

in North America by
Indiana University Press
601 North Morton Street
Bloomington, Indiana 47404-3797
www.iupress.indiana.edu

and in Nigeria by
HEBN Publishers Plc
1 Ighodaro Road, Jericho
P.M.B. 5205
Ibadan, Nigeria
www.hebnpublishers.com

First published in French as
Nollywood: le Phénomène vidéo au Nigeria
sous la direction de Pierre Barrot
© Editions L'Harmattan 2005

Revised English edition © James Currey Ltd 2008
Both editions published with the support of
the Embassy of France in Nigeria

Liberté · Égalité · Fraternité
RÉPUBLIQUE FRANÇAISE

1 2 3 4 5 12 11 10 09 08

British Library Cataloguing in Publication Data
Nollywood : the video phenomenon in Nigeria
  1. Video recordings - Production and direction - Nigeria
  2. Motion pictures - Nigeria - History
1. Barrot, Pierre
791.4'3'0232'09669

ISBN 978-1-84701-505-1 (James Currey cloth)
ISBN 978-1-84701-504-4 (James Currey paper)
ISBN 978-978-081-2096 (HEBN paper)

Cataloging information available from the Library of Congress
ISBN 978-0-253-35352-8 (Indiana casebound)
ISBN 978-0-253-22117-9 (Indiana paper)

Typeset in 10/12 pt Photina with Compacta bold display
by Long House, Cumbria

Printed and bound in Malaysia

Contents

List of Illustrations

Photographs

Tables

Figure

List of Film Profiles
compiled & written by Pierre Barrot

Notes on Contributors

Franck Baku Fuita graduated from the Kinshasa School of Journalism. Since 1988 he has worked for the weekly newspaper *La Semaine*, and later at the daily *La Référence-Plus*. He was a correspondent for the Press agency SYFIA as well as for the Central African media news bulletin for the Panos Institute in Paris.

Olivier Barlet has published a number of translations of books on Africa or by African writers, and has written a wide range of books, most notably *Les Cinémas d'Afrique noir*. A member of the French Union of Film Critics, he runs the film pages of the periodicals *Afrique-Asie* and *Continental*. From 1997 to 2004 he was editor of the magazine *Africultures* and still runs the *Africultures* website which publishes many papers on African film (www.africultures.com). He is also involved with the African Federation of Film Critics and contributes to their website (www.africine.org).

Pierre Barrot worked as a journalist in Benin, then as a producer of the television series *Taxi Brousse* (which won the Human Rights Award at the 'Vues d'Afrique' film festival in Montréal 2001 and the Award of the Best Series at the 'Cinéma tout-écran' film festival, Geneva, 2003). He co-wrote (with Seydou Drame) the novel *Bill l'espiègle* (Lieu commun, 1993). After 11 years living in West Africa, four of which as the Regional audiovisual attaché of the Embassy of France in Nigeria, he is now the French cultural attaché in Algiers.

Godefroid Bwiti Lumisa graduated from the Kinshasa School of Journalism. Formerly News editor of the daily newspaper *La Référence Plus*, he now runs the News agency InterCongo media, and is Editor-in-chief of the SYFIA press agency for the Great Lakes area.

Ibbo Daddy Abdoulaye graduated in English from the University of Niamey and later became became Niger's correspondent for the Press Agency SYFIA, and editor of the monthly review *Les Echos du Sahel*. In 2004 he won the Lorenzo Natali prize, awarded by the European Union to journalists involved in human rights and development issues.

Notes on Contributors

Tunde Kelani was trained at the London Film School in the 1970s, and has been Director of Photography on numerous Nigerian films. In 1986 he produced and filmed *Iwa* directed by Lola Fani-Kayode. The *White Handkerchief*, a short film co-produced with the South African company M-Net, was his first experience of directing. His full-length films have all been shot on video: *Ti Oluwa Nile* (I, II and III) on Hi 8; *Kosseegbe* on VHS; *Oleku* (I and II) on DV; *Ayo Ni Mofe* (I and II) on S-VHS and eight subsequent films on DVCam: *Thunderbolt, Saworoide, Agogo Eewo, The Campus Queen, Efunsetan, Abeni* (I and II) and *The Narrow Path*). Tunde Kelani's work was the subject of a special retrospective during the New York African Film Festival in 2004.

Frédéric Noy is a photographer, journalist and video producer, and he worked as a stills photographer on several French feature films. He has lived in Tanzania, where he published *Being 20 in Dar es Salaam* (Editions Charles-Léopold Mayer, Alternatives, 2001), in Nigeria and more recently in the Sudan.

Don Pedro Obaseki produced and directed such films as *Land of the Living Dead* and *Igodo*. He also wrote the play *The Bridge at the Fiesta*. Don Pedro Obaseki created and chaired the Filmmakers Cooperative of Nigeria.

Ogova Ondego graduated in Communication and is now a journalist for the Kenyan cultural press agency ComMatters, specializing in cultural news. He is also a correspondent for the newsletter *Africa Film & Television* and a member of the organizing committee of the Nairobi African Film Week.

Tunde Oladunjoye, freelance journalist, graduated from the Nigerian Institute of Journalism. Head of the Centre for Media Education and Networking in Lagos and member of the board of trustees of Ogun State Radio, he is also a poet and coordinated the publication of *Activist Poets* in Lagos (2002).

Preface

Pierre Barrot

Even to begin writing about video production in Nigeria is a challenge for one simple reason: according to the most conservative estimates, around 9,000 full-length features have been filmed in this country between 1992 and the beginning of 2007. For the sake of convenience we will refer to these as 'films', even though they are outside the commercial industry's structure. Over the fifteen years studied, Nigeria was ranked second in the world for the overall number of 'films' produced (below India and above the United States). Yet 'the Nigerian audio-visual industry', or more flamboyantly 'Nollywood', as it is called by the local professionals, produces works only in the medium of video, and with budgets that are absurdly low in comparison to those of other continents.

The total production costs of some 1,600 Nigerian films made in 2006 is estimated to be less than US$ 60 million, and is thus lower than the budget of a single Hollywood film.[1] Put another way, it is hardly more than the amount paid by media mogul Rupert Murdoch at the end of 2004 for his apartment in Manhattan.[2]

Thus, economic significance has less to do with what makes the Nigerian video industry so impressive (even though it is said to employ some 200,000 people). On the contrary, it is the very fact that its production budgets are so modest and its very character so prolific and 'industrious'. Even if one puts aside the multiple re-makes, sequels and plagiarisms, there are still 9,000 films telling thousands of stories that speak to an audience of millions across the African continent.

This gargantuan production of video-films constitutes a social, economic and cultural phenomenon without precedent. It is culture that is not the reserve of the so-called 'cultured classes'. Aside from the music industry, there has never been any other aspect of African culture that has resonated in such a way, achieved such a high profile and above all made such a big impact on the population.

In terms of the film content, it would be unrealistic to attempt an exhaustive study, even if such an exercise was worth the considerable effort required – most of the works in question could be seen as 'disposable', destined to be seen once and quickly forgotten. The more

1. The average budget of a Hollywood feature film exceeded the sum of US$ 100 million in 2003 (US$ 102.8 million, of which US$ 63.8 million were production costs and US$ 39 million were for distribution), according to Jack Valenti, President of the Motion Picture Association of America. A Nigerian feature film therefore costs the equivalent of six seconds of an American film.
2. US$ 44 million paid in cash (Satellifax, Paris, 20 December 2004).

important question is how to find a sure path through the morass of films on offer.

The contributors to this book can only speak from personal experience and individual taste on the subject. In fact it is impossible to know whether the hundred or so films cited in this study (including the thirteen films which are profiled in some detail) make up a truly fair sample. The choice of films included in their analysis was at times related to the artistic, or at times simply the commercial qualities which made them stand out from the rest. In other cases it was a word of mouth recommendation or simply a chance encounter with a particular film. It is quite likely that many better or more important films have been neglected. Please note that all footnotes in the book are written by the editor and not by the individual contributors.

This book does not aspire to be a complete academic analysis of the industry nor a comprehensive work of reference for well-informed film buffs. Besides, up until 2006, Nigeria remained completely outside of the world of international cinematographic creation and production. The aim of the contributors to this book is to present a series of accounts that bear witness to a number of different engagements with the industry and to explore a phenomenon which remains largely unrecognized, particularly outside of Africa. The industry justifiably arouses much curiosity due to its prolific activity and partly because of the unique way in which the films are produced and distributed.

Which other country has seen the birth of a visual media industry so autonomous and so able to sustain and reproduce itself? The Nigerian 'video industry' might still have an image of being fly-by-night but fifteen years after its emergence, its continued growth and incredible popular success prove that its foundations are solid and its future secure.

Opposite: Retailer in Ikoyi,
Lagos, 2007
(© Robert Minangoy)

1 'Video is the AIDS of the Film Industry'
Pierre Barrot

Niamey, Niger, February 2004. At this time of year, the dry harmattan wind from the desert brings with it a portion of dust by day and by evening a breath of fresh air. At the foot of the hill the river flows slowly past and conjures images from its depths. You might even expect a glimpse of the mythical old hippopotamus of Jean Rouch's early ethnographic films.[1]

A few hundred metres from the river, the French-Niger Cultural Centre (referred to as 'le Franco') is having a week-long retrospective of cinema from Niger. On the evening of 20 February it is the turn of the director Djingarey Maïga to screen two of his feature films: *Aube noire* and *Vendredi noir*. The programme and the mood are fitting, as two days earlier Jean Rouch had died in a car accident on the Zinder road, just a few hours after a standing ovation from the audience at 'le Franco'.

Emotions ran high as some of the filmmakers present spoke of the huge loss of the man considered the 'father of Niger's film industry'. Djingarey Maïga paid homage to the master and quoted Rouch's declaration that 'video is the AIDS of the film industry'. Now that he is gone, one can only guess at his meaning: was he warning about the viral nature of piracy, which is frequently associated with video, or making a point about the rapid proliferation of video-players? Or perhaps he was warning of the dangers of this equipment, since video, as a tool designed for mass consumption, was beginning to replace film, previously the preserve of a small group of specialists? Such purists might fear the process of vulgarization and compare it to a weakening in an immuno-defence system – a virus that could no doubt be considered equally fatal to cinema.

At the time of this retrospective, the film industry in Niger seemed as good as finished. After the death of Jean Rouch, the French-Niger Cultural Centre was the last remaining venue in Niamey showing films. 'Jangorzo', the only commercial cinema, occasionally received films for screening, but mostly videos. Cinematic production in Niger had practically ceased; the last film released was Djingarey Maïga's *Vendredi noir* in 2000.

1. In his documentary film *Bataille sur le grand fleuve* (1951), Jean Rouch, at that time a young ethnographic film-maker, followed a hunt of mythic proportions, in which the hero was a hippopotamus that was never seen, never caught, but omnipresent and unforgettable.

Pierre Barrot

It could be said that cinema in Niger, as in many other African countries, had been killed off by video, the virus identified by Jean Rouch.[2] Pirate video-clubs flourish these days, as in most other parts of Africa. It is also true that the public have got out of the habit of watching films on the big screen in the darkened halls of picture houses, which is not surprising given the dilapidated state of the cinemas, the general wear and tear on the fittings that had turned the cinematic experience into something of an ordeal. Looking back to the screening of a film in a commercial cinema in Niamey in 1992, the building itself hadn't quite hit its all time low, but even then the audience had to strain to make out the pale image on the dusty screen, tolerate interference from the crackly sound projection and put up with frequent breaks when the film reel snapped.

In March 2004, some weeks after Jean Rouch's death, his documentary *Les maîtres fous* (winner of an award in Venice in 1957) was screened in Ghana, where it had been made. At this time, despite the fact that Ghana was a much wealthier and more populated country than Niger, it had not had a single functioning cinema for several years. The screening of *Les maîtres fous* was organized by the Goethe Institute in Accra and was watched mainly by students of the local film school. After a few minutes, the film came off its tracks, the old 16mm stock having strayed off its sprockets. The reel jammed and with an inexperienced, or absent, projectionist the film was destroyed in a slow inexorable dissolving on the screen as the celluloid burned. It all seems a long way from the passion for cinema which was conjured up in the scene of the fire in the projectionist's room in *Cinema paradiso*.[3]

This passion for visual images does still exist in Africa, but due partly to the run-down state of the large cinemas, it has been transferred to the local video industry. In 2004, at last, a revival in African film seemed possible thanks to the 'Africa Cinemas' programme.[4] The Burkinabe feature film *Moi et mon blanc* was the first African film to be brought to the audiences of Niamey. Ironically, Pierre Yameogo's film ends in the happy childhood setting of an old video-club with a mere FCFA 50 entrance fee[5] where pirated copies of old westerns are shown to the great joy of the spectators. If video is a kind of virus, then its victims seemed to be embracing it.

At the Niamey gathering in February 2004, Djingarey Maïga was very critical of video as a medium, despite his frustrations with 16mm film: the acrobatics he had to go through to get hold of film stock, the miracles needed in order to start filming and eventually to be able to release the work. A few years previously he had faced humiliation when his film *Vendredi noir* was overlooked by the 2001 selection committee of FESPACO (Festival Panafricain du Cinéma de Ouagadougou), only to be 'rediscovered' and then be screened upside-down as the reels had been set up incorrectly. He had plenty to complain about,

2. Jean Rouch, inventor of cinema direct is also considered to be one of the precursors to French 'New Wave' (Nouvelle Vague) cinema. After a long career in Africa he was President of Cinemathèque française (French Film Archive) from 1986 to 1991.
3. *Cinema Paradiso* (1988) was directed by Italian filmmaker Giuseppe Tornatore.
4. This rescue plan was aimed at relaunching the distribution of African films across Africa. Financed jointly by the European Union, France and the Agence de la Francophonie, it produced such disappointing results that it was abandoned.
5. FCFA 50 = US$ 0.016 at the time of writing.

but Djingarey Maïga was resolute in his rejection of video as a substitute for film, like an old pro under his director's green eye-shade!

However noble and determined this battle cry might sound, the result has been that Niger no longer produces films, and its intransigent filmmakers have decided not to take advantage of video technology as an alternative. This leaves them untainted by the 'inferior' equipment, and moreover leaves audiences in Niger with only imported films to watch. It is no great loss for Niger as it has the good fortune (or misfortune depending on your point of view) to border on one the great video-exporting countries that saturates their market with video-cassettes.

Nigeria, the vast and often misrepresented neighbour of Niger, has become, in just a few years, the world's leading producer of films shot on video. This statistic is unlikely to be taken very seriously by professionals from some other countries and no one can pretend that Nigeria has a great filmmaking tradition, but it produces on average not 500 a year (as in Hollywood), or 800 a year (as in the Bollywood studios of Mumbai), but roughly 1,500 feature films each year. These may be shot on any one of the possible video formats: VHS, Beta, DV, DVCam, Super VHS, DVC-pro and Hi8. This represents an average of 30 new films each week. These are not short films, for they last anywhere between 90 minutes and three hours, and they are flooding the larger markets of Idumota in Lagos, Onitsha in the Niger Delta and others across sub-Saharan Africa. Anglophone African countries were the first to experience this influx, but now even francophone Africa can't escape – Yoruba language films are all the rage from Cotonou to Porto Novo, and those made in English have audiences in Lomé, Kinshasa and even Dakar.

On her way through Cameroon in 2002, the Nigerian superstar Geneviève Nnaji had to disguise herself with a headscarf to escape the mob of fans on the streets of Douala. Niger has not only been invaded by Nigerian video films but submerged by them (see Ibbo Daddy Abdoulaye on this phenomenon, pp. 97–104). Nigerian films are simultaneously aired on television, in theatres, in video-clubs and on domestic video-players. Critics don't hesitate to call this an epidemic.

Invasive by nature, video has undermined cinema across Africa at many levels. In Cotonou, the video-club pirates base their programming closely on those of the cinemas and take advantage of the trailers for forthcoming films.[6] Instead of going to see the original film in mediocre cinematic conditions, audiences choose to watch even poorer quality versions of pirated video copies at a fraction of the cost.

Jean Rouch was right about one thing, video, and its companion, piracy, are certainly contributing to the decline or, in some countries such as Ghana and Niger, to the last gasps of the African picture houses.

6. Interview with Janvier Yahouedeou, a video distributor from Benin, December 2003.

Pierre Barrot

What is happening to African film production? Francophone sub-Saharan Africa (comprising 18 countries) produced only 12 films in 2001 and 2002.[7] This can't really be blamed on piracy or the video industry. Since when has the production of African films depended on their distribution in African cinemas? Even the most popular films have largely been financed by external film funds such as the Fonds Sud, the Fonds Francophone, the European Union's ACP programme and various television channels such as TV5 or Canal France International. This might surprise people but it is true – the presence or absence of an audience in African cinemas has practically no effect on the local production of films. Moreover, this is not a new development: with or without video, and with or without piracy, an African film made on celluloid has no hope of covering its production costs with receipts from African cinemas.[8]

The production of so few films for African cinemas is not caused by video – it goes on regardless. Conversely, the fact so many films are produced in Nigeria today can certainly be said to be thanks to video. It is also the case that cinematic filmmaking in Nigeria only existed for a short period of time, appearing as late as 1970 and being pretty much finished by the 1980s. Françoise Balogun's book *Le cinema du Nigeria* (1984),[9] described a film industry which 'barely born, was already showing signs of its own demise'.

In contrast to the few dozen celluloid films shot since 1970 in Nigeria, all laboriously executed, poorly distributed, rarely acknowledged by the critics[10] and given very little international recognition, there are 9,000 video-films, distributed in numerous countries, and watched by millions of viewers. A few are even acknowledged by European and American film festivals. If cinematic filmmaking has a chance of recovery in Nigeria today,[11] then it will be partly thanks to the market opened up during the feverish years of video production. In this way, video has really given the country an opportunity.

It is tempting to suggest that in francophone Africa so *few* video-films have been made *because* of the existence of a cinematic tradition. However commendable the conventions and habits of filmmaking might be, they still weigh heavily on the conception, budgets and schedules of all productions, including video. In 2003, the French Ministry of Foreign Affairs received 36 proposals requesting financial support through Fonds Sud, of which they took on seven. It is interesting to compare these proposals' projected budgets in relation to the length of the films in minutes. The project with the largest budget came from Burkina Faso, the beacon of sub-Saharan African filmmaking, at 10,769 Euros per minute. This would be a typical budget for cinematic production, but this film was to be shot on video. The lowest budget proposal came in from Nigeria at 222 Euros per minute, ie fifty times less costly. The Burkinabe film director with the highest budget

7. Interview with Baba Hama, general delegate of FESPACO, *Jeune Afrique/L'intelligent*, 26 January 2003.
8. The same could be said for French films. In 2003, only three out of more than 200 films paid off their production costs through income from French cinemas alone. But these films also had other sources of revenue on the national market through television broadcasting rights and video editions.
9. Editions L'Harmattan, 1984, Cinemedia series, *Cinemas d'Afrique noire*.
10. Ola Balogun is alone in enjoying a certain international prestige (including in the French-speaking world). Françoise Balogun (1984) has written that 'it is difficult in some ways to defend Nigerian cinema, but it is impossible not to respect and admire people who work in at times unsustainable conditions out of a love for what they do.'
11. The Fespaco grand prix for 2007 was awarded for the first time to a Nigerian film director, Newton Aduaka (who lives in France), for his film *Ezra*, shot in Rwanda. In Nigeria three new cinema complexes opened up in Lagos between 2004 and 2006.

was a new director, not known by the industry. In contrast, the Nigerian film director presenting the lowest budget was considered to be one of the most active film directors in the country – Tunde Kelani, 59 years old, a graduate of the London Film School and honoured at a number of film festivals. Unlike his Burkinabe colleague, Tunde Kelani has developed a production method adapted to the economic conditions in Nigeria, aimed at mass audiences and the local video market, even though his films still enjoy international recognition on the film festival circuit.

One of the many video shops that distribute V-CDs in Lagos

(© Robert Minangoy)

Returning to Niamey and the 20 February event at which Djingarey Maïga delivered his diatribe against video: when he showed his 1983 film *Aube noir*, there were even more technical blunders (such as poor cuts and splicing) than one finds in most contemporary Nigerian videos. Badly built sets were another problem along with a general lack of competence or aestheticism in the image itself. Other faults included poor acting (Maïga himself acknowledged the difficulty of finding actors in Niger able to act well in French). At one level these criticisms are not important, as the essential quality of the film, its strength, comes from the director's sincerity and his authentic portrayal of the central themes of polygamy and arranged marriage. This is also true of his film *Vendredi noir*, which chronicles the commonplace murder of a woman, victim of a violent husband.

Those who would criticize the melodrama of this film don't need to look far to see that it is about lived realities, not creative or artistic fantasies. A few steps from the auditorium and adjoining the 'Franco' bar area is a small eating place run by a vivacious woman, who has not seen either of Djingarey Maïga's films and whose clients are too hungry to give him much thought. Her countenance changes when she stares at a tall, gaunt-looking man who is walking past and she lets slip that he has killed his wife. Faced with a disbelieving audience she recounts the story of a dreadful crime, vaguely disguised as an accident. If her story is to be believed, the man had not even bothered to give a convincing account of what happened. He was never really challenged by the traditional social order and even those who thought it was more than an unfortunate incident didn't denounce him.

It is precisely in order to challenge aspects of society that disgust him that Djingarey Maïga makes films. Even though *Vendredi noir*[12] was co-produced by a French organization called Village Films and has a technical and artistic merit that was absent from *Aube noire*, the two films are similar in that the director's message is more important than its artistic ambitions. The story surpasses the style. 'Too bad', according to Laurent Mareschal, French promoter of the Three Continents Festival, when talking about Nigerian films that there isn't a 'hint of innovation in their form'.

Indeed, at the time of their screening in Niamey, Djingarey Maïga's films immediately brought to mind a Nigerian video-film called *The Apple*, directed by Lancelot Imasuen and shown a year earlier at a festival in Benin.[13] As in Maïga's films there were no stylistic flourishes, but a story that rang true and actors who gave life to their characters, as well as a dramatic tension truer to the realities of the scene than to the contrivances of a film script. This film might resonate with Djingarey Maïga. It uses his approach of fearlessly confronting society's ills (in this case the marriage of very young girls), it is sincere, and has the same kind of impact, due to its underlying concern for simplicity and directness. Between the filmmaker from Niger, who had to wait eight to ten years between making each new feature film, and the Nigerian 'home-video' craftsman, prolific and frenetic in his serial approach to shooting films, there is common ground, both visually on the screen and above all in their shared concern for the audience.

Djingarey Maïga may have made a tactical error in denouncing video – this might well prevent him from making the many other films that he has in his head and that will never come to light if he continues to be burdened with traditional filmmaking techniques.

12. *Vendredi noir* was awarded a medal at the Angers festival in 2001.
13. Produced by Videofield, the company owned by Emmanuel Isikaku, who was at that time president of the Society of Nigerian Video Distributors.

Of the 1,500 Nigerian video-films produced each year, a great number are without doubt unworthy of attention, but at least those that do deserve some scrutiny are in the public domain. They would have had no hope in a system where the obsession with the full cinematic product demands technical and financial thresholds so high that they bring the industry to an almost complete standstill. Niger, as noted above, may host retrospectives of a filmmaker's work, but it no longer produces anything new. Nigeria on the other hand has very little that it can submit to the film festival circuit but it is satisfying the need of many African people for images of their own lives. Nigerian videos are portraying the fantasies, dreams, fears, doubts, hatreds and enthusiasms of a country that is so large[14] that much of the rest of the continent seems to be able to find itself in there somewhere. They may not be worthy of the Cannes Film Festival, but they are certainly worth watching.

14. A population of 140 million, according to the 2006 Census. 133 million according to a 2004 World

Film Profile No. 1
The Apple
Directed by Lancelot Imasuen

Date of release: 2000
Production Company: Cecilian Pictures
Filmscript: Adim Williams
Producer: Theodore Anyanji
Cast: Chioma Onwuka, Tony Umez, Peter Bunor, Rita Nzela & Florence Onuma

Uju, a fifteen year old girl, is in love with Arinze who is twice her age. The young girl's father is against the relationship and thinks that she is too young to marry. He tries to separate them by any means he can, even resorting to beating up his daughter. His wife tries to make him relent but he is adamant. In desperation Uju runs away with her lover. Her parents put out a missing persons announcement and eventually she returns to the house, persuaded that her father will let her marry Arinze, as he has promised her on the phone. But as soon as he has his daughter back, the father goes back to his previous objections. It takes Uju's suicide attempt for him to realize that in the end he has lost this battle. So Uju and Arinze are happily married, but this is a Nigerian video, so the plot veers away from a fairy-tale ending into Greek tragedy.

Uju is so young that sexual intercourse with Arinze is painful and soon causes problems between the newly-weds. Out of her depth, the girl finds herself unable to play wife or mistress of the house in the way her husband expects. The girl's lack of maturity begins to trouble Arinze who loses his temper. After a violent domestic scene, Uju assumes she will be able to take refuge in her parent's house, but the older couple have suffered so much from her obstinacy that her sudden change of mind isn't met with much enthusiasm. Uju and Arinze have a temporary reconciliation, but each day that passes persuades Arinze that Uju is really just a child. As the atmosphere in their house becomes increasingly suffocating, he spends more and more time away from home. One day, Uju locks the door and prevents him from coming back in, and when she finally relents, he gives her a severe beating to teach her a lesson. The young girl yet again takes refuge with her parents but her father's sarcasm soon drives her away. Returning to her husband, she finds him with a mistress. Despite this incident there is a period of respite during which Uju becomes pregnant. But when the baby arrives it is still-born, and after the delivery Uju suffers from a vaginal tear. (This affliction, quite common in Africa among girls who marry at a very young age or who have been excised, can cause incontinence, which is hard for any couple to

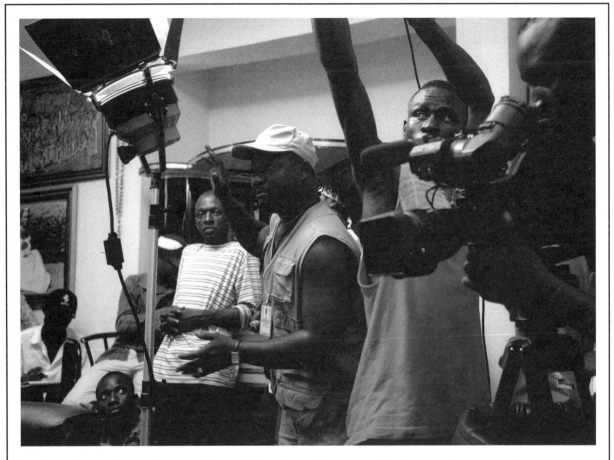

bear). Uju's condition disgusts Arinze. Rejected and desperate Uju is taken in by her parents, but they cannot stop her committing suicide.

The Apple (possibly a metaphor for 'green fruit') is a real melodrama. Its technical quality leaves a lot to be desired and the actors' performances are sometimes strained, but the leading role, played by the young Chioma Onwuka, making her debut in this film, is very convincing. The cinematography is effective, and the plot, while credible, doesn't give the audience any respite as it moves from one hellish situation to the next. Although it pushes a very particular message, the film is never didactic in style. *The Apple* is a perfect example of the kind of drama that characterizes Nigerian video.

The director of this film, Lancelot Oduwa Imasuen was 33 years old at the time of writing. He has produced and directed more than 70 films (including sequels). This impressive figure does not mean that the work is slipshod. One of the films that he directed (starring Stephanie Okereke), was screened at the 2004 African Film Festival in New York.

Lancelot Imasuen directing at a shoot in Lagos
(© Frédéric Noy)

2 'The Italians of Africa'
Pierre Barrot

Lagos. Among the stream of vehicles crossing the lagoon at Eko bridge tens of yellow minibuses (*danfos*), packed with passengers, race across to 'the mainland', leaving behind the skyscrapers of Lagos Island – the banks, the billboards advertising mobile phones and the forest of antennae. Near the entrance to the National Stadium they are joined by larger buses (*molwes*) which are not allowed onto the islands of Victoria and Lagos, protecting the business quarter and fashionable districts of the city. The *molwes* are one of the more fantastical elements of this Nigerian metropolis: steel monsters grafted together from the cabin and chassis of a Mercedes lorry or a 1970s Mack truck, joined at the back end to the body of a Nigerian-built bus. Even more disconcerting are the lorries that transport the workers in and out of the city – towed containers with steel tops perforated by a series of large holes. Workers are packed into these 'cattle trucks' shoulder to shoulder as they travel to the factory or building site.

As one gets further away from the islands and hits the bottlenecks at each crossroad or junction, the traffic becomes increasingly dense and noisy. Western Avenue is one of the motorways that acts like a drainage channel for the city's congestion. It is generally thought that 12 million people live in this city, but the exact number is not known – it could be anything between 8 and 15 million.

As drivers approach Surulere, there is one building that stands out because of the huge billboard covering its four-storey façade and advertising the film *Dangerous Twins*, Two larger than life characters are displayed, with London Bridge in the background – they are both played by one of Nigeria's video superstars, Ramsay Nouah. Down towards the next roundabout, pasted up on the supporting pillars of a bridge, are hundreds of small posters announcing another batch of new films. They have bold, aggressive designs for their modest size – mainly of faces, some grimacing, with mouths twisted in pain, others seductive and alluring, smiling at you with ultra-white teeth. This expressionistic portrait gallery is there to catch the attention of the thousands of commuters who plunge into the throng of taxis, buses and *okadas*[1] and thread their way through the street traders hawking

1. Motorbike taxis, named after a now defunct airline company.

their wares in the middle of the road. Just as in Cairo or Mumbai, every night a vast and insatiable audience looks for an escape from the confines of the city without stirring from their homes. This is their own special brand of cinema – full of noise and intensity, high drama and foolish dreams.

Welcome to 'Nollywood' (with 'N' for Nigeria) – making approximately 1,500 films a year, employing 200,000 people and reaching an audience of millions. Lagos is at the forefront of the world's video-film industry, but in contrast to Mumbai, there are no large studios, no projectors or screens, no reels of film and not even a single cinema remaining by 2004. These films are watched at home on the family television through either a VHS or DVD player.

Nollywood films are produced on a small scale and made on the hoof. Three to five days' filming is the average for most of the 'disposable' videos. 'A film that costs 3 million Naira to make on a Monday,' according to video-patriarch Eddie Ugbomah, 'can earn you 10 million Naira by Friday. What other activity in Nigeria can bring such good returns? Not one. This is only possible because the films are a kind of nourishment for people.'[2]

Idumota market, the video bazaar of Lagos; on the poster is Omotola Jalade-Ekeinde, the star of I Have a Dream
(© Jean-Claude Moschetti/REA)

2. Interview given to the 'Nollywood' supplement of *New Age* (5 November 2004). 10 million Naira were then worth US$ 75,000. Eddie Ugbomah, administrator for the Association of Movie Producers, is the creator of over ten feature films made in 16mm and 35mm, and shot in the 1970s to 1980s. He is one of the very few Nigerian filmmakers who have continued their career using video. One of his more recent films *Black Gold* (2005) is shot on video and yet is indistinguishable from his earlier work on celluloid.

Pierre Barrot

V-CD cover of Side Attraction 2,
starring Geneviève Nnaji

Video-editing takes place in the back yards of Surulere where even the kings of the industry work with poor equipment and restricted means amid the noise of generators, Lagos being prone to frequent power cuts. The films are shot in people's houses, or out on the street. The producers are still dreaming of the long-awaited 'film village' (a local *Cinecitta*), promised (but what hasn't he promised?) by the governor of Lagos on a site at Epe, 60 km from the city centre.

To understand how the video industry works in Nigeria you need to go to Idumota market. This vast video-bazaar is best reached on foot from the outskirts of Lagos Island, navigating the crowds and watching out for the small vans and motorbikes that nudge through the jams with hornblasts and bumper scrapes. Eventually you reach a labyrinth of narrow streets, cross the planks of wood that bridge the gutters and climb up the well-worn steps to get to the distributors' covered stalls.

The shops are narrow and packed with customers, and with workers bundling up consignments of cassettes and videos in amongst the general hubbub and blaring soundtracks of the film trailers. These trailers are shown in looped transmission on the store's television screens. The walls are papered from floor to ceiling with posters and video sleeves of a wide range of films: features with gangsters or clergymen (the Bible and the gun turn up frequently, and even, at times, together), Yoruba sagas, comic sketches, 'juju films' (about witchcraft), Hausa musical comedies and dramas inspired by real life events.

Mostly, the posters follow a certain formula: it is rare, for example, to see the actors' names – their faces speak for themselves. Everybody knows the stars such as Geneviève Nnaji, Omotola, Stephanie Okereke, Jim Iyke, Ramsey Nouah, Nkem Owoh, so there is no need for an introduction. As with American movie posters it is also rare for the director's name to be very obvious. The producer is also quite discreet. It is the distributor that is headlined: Videofield, Infinity, Grand Touch, Ezee. The larger distributors come mainly from the South-east of Nigeria. Emmanuel Isikaku, owner of Videofield, was former president of the Nigerian Association of Distributors. When a group of producers and directors, formed a 'cooperative of filmmakers' and wanted to break away from the control that Idumota market held over the sale of video-cassettes, Isikaku just laughed at them. The cooperative did manage to set up its own, well-organized market in the district of Surulere where many of the producers are based, yet Idumota market continues to be central to the trade. Despite general disorder and dilapidation, the Nigerian film industry is certainly thriving there.

The distributors do not restrict themselves to distribution. Often they are the ones who direct the directors, providing them with a leading actor, a spicy story, or an advance to get them started. On top, there is a draconian schedule for shooting. This industry has a very rapid turnover of revenue. Competition is fierce and the fear of piracy makes it essential to get the films out as soon as possible. The distributors' aim is to recoup their investment before the video-pirates, the plagiarists or simply the 're-make' artists get hold of the plot and the characters. A few weeks after the triumphant launch of the previously mentioned *Dangerous Twins*, the same Ramsey Nouah appeared in a re-hash of the same story called *London Boy*. When Tunde Kelani completed his film *The Campus Queen*, one of his actors was quick to cook up a Yoruba version, without any regard for the issues of copyright. And just before the well-publicized launch of Kingsley Ogoro's film *Across the Niger*, one cunning opportunist changed the name of his film at the eleventh hour to *Across the River*, hoping to trick unthinking consumers into buying the wrong film.

The sheer volume of films being made is in response to the insatiable appetite of the audiences – the Nigerian public is passionate about these locally produced films, and they keep asking for more. A study of audiences conducted by the Gallup-Nigeria Institute in 2003 revealed that 67 per cent of homes in the urban areas had either VHS or V-CD

Pierre Barrot

THE Campus Queen

A TUNDE KELANI Film

Two posters for Tunde Kelani's The Campus Queen

players. Most of these machines were hardly ever used to record programmes from television, but largely to satisfy the sudden hunger of Nigerian audiences for locally made video films. This phenomenon is even more striking when compared to the music industry, which, at least in the south of the country, is dominated by output from the USA. All day long the FM radio stations pump out the sound of American rap. Again this contrasts with francophone Africa where local rhythms dominate the air waves – Congolese *ndombolo*,

Cameroonian *makossa* and *zouglou* from Côte d'Ivoire. On the other hand, in francophone Africa, it is imported images that sell on a grand scale: video shops and clubs, cinemas and television screens show mostly American films, or Brazilian and Mexican soap operas. In Nigeria the situation is quite different.

Nigeria was an unlikely place for this exponential growth in film-making, as cinema only appeared in the country quite recently. After a first experiment by a Lebanese producer and director (with a film called

Son of Africa), it was an American, Ossie Davis who encouraged film as art, through his association with the future Nobel Prizewinner for Literature, Wole Soyinka. The first proper feature film to make its appearance was his *Kongi's Harvest* (1970). Ola Balogun is the only Nigerian filmmaker to have established an international reputation, partly thanks to his training in France. He also opened the way for popular cinema; first with *Ajani Ogun*, and then through his brief association with the Yoruba theatre performer Hubert Ogunde. In the same era, Eddie Ugbomah made mediocre films on minimal budgets. But while Ola Balogun stopped making feature films in the 1980s in order to concentrate on documentary filmmaking, Ugbomah moved seamlessly from film to video, which certainly made him one of the precursors of the current home-video 'industry'. The official history of this phenomenon attributes the moment of 'lift-off' to Kenneth Nnebue and Chris Obi Rapu, director and producer respectively, for their film *Living in Bondage* (1992), which sold 200,000 copies.

But Jimi Odumosu, former director of state television in Lagos, tells an anecdote that places the roots of the industry much further back. In 1980, Odumosu was shooting a three-hour long programme for Lagos Television, called *Evil Encounter*, which Odumosu himself described as a horror film. This TV-film told the story of a mother who had wanted a talisman to protect her son who was suffering from difficulties in his professional life. When she went to collect her amulet, the charlatan who had prepared it was out and she picked up another client's amulet by mistake. This turned out to be powerfully malignant, and led to a series of horrible deaths.

This film was promoted extensively before its release. The next morning, as Odumosu made his way from Ikeja (the administrative district of Lagos) to Victoria Island, he discovered that street hawkers at the crossroads were selling video-cassettes of his film, duplicated just after transmission. He learned later that the film was a big seller at Alaba Market, which is still, 27 years on, one of the epicentres of piracy.

Similar stories come out of francophone Africa: the filmmaker Henri Duparc[3] was getting ready for the launch of one of his films on video; the cassettes were due to be released the next day. On his way to a meeting about promoting the event a street seller offered him a video-cassette. To his complete amazement he found that it was his own film, already pirated and distributed around Abidjan.

What is particular about the Nigerian case is that the system of piracy has been adopted by the same producer-distributors who control the video market with such success that they are able continually to re-invest in the production of new films. In this country with the highest population density of all Africa, competition for the vast market has done the rest. The first successful film spawned its own rivals – a whole new and fast-growing industry.

3. Director of the cult film *Bal poussière*, he died in 2006.

How was it possible for a country that had only been responsible for producing a few dozen films for the cinema, to then produce 9,000 video films in just a few years?

There is more than one answer to this, but a contributing factor was probably the pool of exceptional actors. The energy of the Yoruba travelling theatre companies no doubt laid the foundations; Nigerians have also been attributed with a sense of the theatrical. The American journalist Karl Meier once wrote that 'Nigerians are the Italians of Africa.'[4]

But Nigerian videos do not have the light touch of *la comedia dell'arte*. Instead of the humour of Harlequin and Colombine, we find an excess of murder, ritual sacrifice, poisoning, robbery and suicide. If the public is drawn to such macabre stories it is because of their cathartic function in a place which is prey to the power of the spiritual world.

Musician Fela Kuti once characterized the tragedy in the backdrop to the lives of many Nigerians as 'suffering and smiling'. Few countries in the world have endured as much: the blood bath of the 1966 coup (both the Prime Minister and other government ministers were assassinated); the Biafran war with its countless deaths; oil – the poisoned chalice which has created obscene amounts of wealth while leaving the majority of people more poverty stricken than in the 1960s; an explosive cocktail of more than 250 ethnic groups; a propensity for religious fanaticism which spares neither Christians nor Muslims; a level of corruption rarely achieved elsewhere; a succession of dictatorships among which that of Sani Abacha (1994–1998) exceeded all previous records of cruelty and excess.

When democracy was re-established after 1999, there was still a residue of high level violence. This characteristic of Nigerian society permeates many films and is perhaps the key both to why they have had such an impact and to the extraordinarily productive output of the industry. The fear that is created by this violence provides a powerful stimulant to the scriptwriters' imagination. It also contributes to the public's desire for escapism that only fiction can satisfy (the number of documentary films made as a proportion of the overall output is minute).

The violence of this country, whether it is exploited, exaggerated or denounced in film, is not fictional. You only have to approach Lagos from the road that leads from the Benin border to pick up on the atmosphere. Along this 80km route with its 20 or 30 checkpoints, it isn't unusual to come up against a hundred or so police, soldiers or customs officers, armed for the most part with machine guns, sometimes helmeted and wearing bullet-proof vests. At the end of 2004, the Federal Ministry for Police gave out the following bewildering statistic: 15,449 members of the security forces had been killed over a period of four years.[5] The total number of civilian deaths is of course not even known.

4. Author of *This House Has Fallen*, Penguin Books, London, 2001.
5. *Punch*, 29 November 2004.

Pierre Barrot

In 2003, Hammani Tidjani, head of a gang of thieves targeting four-wheel drive cars and operating out of Southern Nigeria, was indicted on 169 counts of murder (115 civilian and 54 police) committed during the theft of 205 vehicles.[6]

Armed bandits in Nigeria have the reputation for merciless killing. The crimes of these 'desperados' seem beyond comprehension. In 2004 in Lagos, one gang tracked a business man who was carrying a large sum of money. He was travelling to the north in an overnight trip by bus when it was chased by two four-wheel drive vehicles. Once they reached the Third Mainland Bridge, an 8 km stretch across the lagoon without street lighting and on which it is impossible to do a U-turn, the bus was machine-gunned and brought to a standstill. Two passengers, picked at random, were shot dead so that the rest, terrified, immediately handed over their valuables. The exact number of victims is not known as many of the passengers may have perished after jumping into the lagoon.

In Ibadan that same year, a flyer was distributed to people living in a middle-class residential area announcing that an attack was going to take place sometime in the next few weeks, and that people should empty their bank accounts and keep the cash in their houses. Those who refused to pay would be executed. Alarmed by this threat the targeted families alerted the police, organized patrols and prepared for the worst, at the same time somewhat sceptical in the face of such audacity. But, at the forewarned time, the gangsters attacked: they took money and valuables and systematically killed those who resisted. Six people died. In Benin city at the end of 2004, one gang killed ten policemen on the same day. The death toll in relation to religious or ethnic conflict is even worse: one estimate gives 53,000[7] as the number of victims between 2001 and 2004, just in the Plateau State region, an area of tension between Christians agriculturalists and Muslim pastoralists.

Contemporary Nigeria provides its scriptwriters with material as exciting as the Wild-West or the prohibition-era films of Hollywood. High levels of insecurity have two effects: not only do they feed production but they also guarantee the outlet for sales. No other country in the world has a market so completely oriented towards domestic consumption. If films in Nigeria are watched almost exclusively at home, to the greater profit of the distributors, it is because people feel safer in their living rooms than going out to a cinema. In any case, in the south of the country cinemas have been closed down one after the other, some converted into warehouses or evangelical churches. There are no doubt many other explanations for these changes but the state of insecurity is key, because it doesn't induce people to go out at night in urban areas which are so vulnerable, and where street lighting is conspicuous by its absence.

6. *New Age,* 11 December 2003.
7. *Daily Trust,* 8 October 2004.

By contrast, in Northern Nigeria, where banditry has never reached the same levels as in the South, cinemas are still open. The revival of Islamic Sharia law has been effective in maintaining the traditional social order. At the Marhaba cinema in Kano, Hausa videos are screened between two Indian musicals. Video-cassettes are on sale at the exit. Even though an audience of hundreds have watched the film for only 50 Naira each (less than 40 US cents), there is still a large 'captive' market of women who buy cassettes (at 250 Naira each) for 'home viewing'. Since the declaration of Sharia law in the year 2000, women no longer have the right to go to the cinema,[8] so, like most of the viewers of the South, these women watch the films at home. In order for many Nigerians to escape their country, they have first to shut themselves up in their living rooms.

8. The prohibitions of Kano State do not specifically forbid women from going to the cinema but do forbid mixed audiences of men and women, so this has led supporters of the prohibitions simply to give up on the female clientele.

Film Profile No. 2
Osuofia in London [Parts I and II]
Directed by Kingsley Ogoro

Date of release: 2003 (Part I) and 2004 (Part II)
Producer-Director: Kingsley Ogoro
Photography: Jonathan Gbemuotor
Filmscript: Emeke Oblakomwa, based on an idea by Kingsley Ogoro
Cast: Nkem Owoh, Mara Dewent, Charles Angiama, Victoria Summers, Cynthia Okereke & Francis Odega

Osuofia is a polygamous farmer from the south-east of Nigeria. Cunning and unsophisticated, he is extremely dishonest when it comes to dealing with complaints from his wives or requests from his neighbours. The day that a representative of the court in Lagos turns up to announce the death of his eldest brother, Osuofia shows no sorrow at the passing of this ungrateful man who left for London years ago without ever getting back in touch. But when Osuofia hears that he had a huge fortune of which he is now the sole inheritor, he is suddenly overcome by a great tenderness for his beloved brother, and orchestrates a great display of tears and emotion, in which his wives also play their part.

Osuofia leaves for London where he has to sign legal documents for the estate. His encounter with 'the city' leads to an avalanche of jokes at his expense: Osuofia is in fact an uncouth country bumpkin and out of his familiar territory he causes quite a stir with his impudent double-dealing. After much wandering, he eventually finds his brother's widow, an attractive, white woman, as sophisticated as they come. Rather nonplussed by her brother-in-law's boorish manner, the young widow has to try to be very casual so as not to arouse Osuofia's suspicions. She is also after the inheritance and needs the brother's signature to secure this, on the advice of a shady Nigerian banker.

Osuofia, who suspects nothing, is soon caught up in the thrill of the grand house, the butler, the sumptuous limousine and especially the widow who his brother has bequeathed to him - he is convinced, in accordance with the law of his home area, that the Englishwoman is part of his inheritance.

After a series of unlikely turns of fortune, Osuofia uncovers the banker's plot and somehow achieves a complete turnaround in the young widow, with whom he runs away to Nigeria. The sequel (*Osuofia in London*, Part II) deals with his triumphant marriage back in the village, and with the marital problems of the Englishwoman, who is unaccustomed to pounding yam with a pestle or dealing with the mischief-making of a bunch of co-wives.

This film is probably the most successful of all Nigerian video-films.

Its first public screening in front of 2,000 people in Lagos brought in more money than *The Lord of the Rings* on the day of its simultaneous release in the cinemas of Nairobi. Following the screening, some 300,000 to 400,000 VHS-cassettes and V-CDs were in circulation.

After the film was released, the actor Nkem Owoh became part of the 'Big Five' (ie the five most well-paid actors in Nollywood). He was later in a series of quite unsuccessful films, but no matter which role he played from then on, as an actor he was always referred to as 'Osuofia'.

Despite impressive direction, striking sets and props, clever editing (such as in the scene where Osuofia tries to kill an antelope) and its reputation as a high-class Nigerian production, *Osuofia in London* is all in all a very low budget film. The animated pictures used in the opening credits look amateurish. Some scenes on location in the heart of London seem to be shot in one take without any rehearsal.

The success of *Osuofia in London* is rooted not only in the quality of the directing, and in the comic genius of Nkem Owoh, but also in that it is one of the rare Nigerian films which is universal in its appeal, popular with both adults and children.

3 Stress Warriors
Pierre Barrot

As an actor, my whole life is dedicated to you. Do you really think that the pittance that they pay me can compensate for the amount of creative energy that I put into each one of the films that I make? You can never pay for creativity at its true value. How can you quantify the happiness that I bring to people? In hospitals, houses and schools they enjoy watching me. It comforts them. Do you know what stress can do to people? It can kill them. It reduces their life expectancy. And as an artist, I fight stress. I make you laugh, I remove the signs of stress from your face and I increase your life expectancy. Can you put a price on this? You can never pay me enough for that![1]

Lanre Balogun, the actor who spoke these words, could be accused of being pretentious, but he isn't. Not only is he a remarkable actor[2] but the stress which he talks about is a core ingredient of Nigerian life. Jimi Odumosu, director and owner of the Lagos Television channel makes similar claims:

Many Nigerians die of stress. Going to the cinema is the best cure for stress that I know, you escape the real world, you become less tense, you feel better.

Even if watching films does help to combat stress in Nigeria, the films themselves are steeped in it. Anyone who takes Nigerian film as a point of reference for other African cinemas will be surprised. Filmmakers in the Sahel (Burkina Faso, Mali and Senegal), the most prolific on the continent, have familiarized their public with a style of filming often contemplative,[3] imbued with the oral tradition and sometimes very lyrical. People have even discussed the 'aesthetic of the slow pace'. There is nothing of this in Nigerian video. Watching the adverts on television for the week's forthcoming films is enough to dispel any thoughts of such slow-moving films. Staccato editing, a rush of special effects, jerky camera movements, striking close-up shots, thundering voiceover sales pitches and deafening music. To grab the harassed buyer's attention and do down the competition from

1. Interview given for the Nollywood supplement of *New Age*, May 2004.
2. See the reviews lavished on the films *Dangerous Twins* and *Thunderbolt*.
3. Gaston Kabore's film *Buud Yam* (premiered at Fespaco, 1997) is a good example of this. The plot is thin: it serves as a pretext for a road-movie through the main regions and varied cultures of Burkina. This film had a huge popular success in its own country (approximately 500,000 tickets sold at the cinemas).

dozens of distributors, you have to hit hard. The films have to capture the viewers' imagination.

This 'American style' is not found in every film, however. Hausa videos are generally less charged, and if there is any element of suspense, it comes in short bursts. The main influence is Indian cinema rather than American 'B' movies.

Even if the cinematic frames of reference are not the same in the North as in the South, in both cases it is the production styles of popular cinema which are being exploited (Indian melodramas, karate films, westerns and gangster movies). Watching a video-film from Southern Nigeria, there is not a trace of aestheticism or poetry, but one can certainly find pace, energy and a continuing concern for the dramatic. 'Teasing' the audience is the golden rule: from the opening scene of *The Addict* (by Fred Amata), a drug-addict son slashes his mother with a broken bottle; from that point on the story is told in flashback. The same pattern is followed in *Hit the Street* (by Chico Ejiro) with the film beginning with a murder, followed by the suicide of the heroine. In *Saving Alero* (by Tade Ogidan), death threats at the end of a trial set up the dramatic tension. The audience is gripped and not let off the hook until the last scene – perhaps not even then. In the final frames the heroine, Alero (played by Uche Obi-Osotule), is condemned to death by a village tribunal and thrown into a lake. The viewer concludes that she has drowned, which is confirmed by words in the closing credits on the martyring of widows in Africa. But just at the point when all you can hope for is that the screen will go black, there is a final twist: Alero resurfaces, choking; she will be saved at the eleventh hour.

When Nigerian feature films are discussed, the word 'drama' comes up repeatedly. It is clear that it is not the fictional nature of the stories that is important (poetic and dream-like situations barely feature at all)[4] but the dramatic intensity, and the amount of tension generated.

Drama and spectacle are dominant features of Nigerian films – and these are the key ingredients of popular cinema more generally. Even though drama can nearly always be conjured up, spectacle is another story and demands expenditure not always within the tight budgets of the Nigerian producers and distributors. It may be a profusion of technical effects at the bottom end of the scale (thunderbolts striking down the wicked; magic beams of light, ghostly visions, devils superimposed on the image); or morphing effects (changing a person into an antelope, as in the film *Sango*, for example). Another technique is trick-editing such as when the protagonist of *Osuofia in London* shoots an antelope (clearly cut in from a wildlife film); or the helicopters in Zeb Ejiro's *The President Must not Die* (borrowed from archive footage and never shown landing or connecting with the action of the film). Similarly in Ladi Ladebo's film *Heritage* – the helicopter is framed to see

4. The supernatural, by contrast, is a key element which is understood by many in the audience as a real presence and is therefore not classified as being in the 'realms of the imaginary'.

25

only the blades in close-up, even though the action is about taking on board a smuggler with his stolen art treasures.

In *Dangerous Twins*, Ramsey Nouah, supposedly visiting London with his English wife is in fact alone on the screen in all the street scenes. His wife appears only in a tightly cropped shot and in interior shots (she would have stayed in her hotel room if the production budget only allowed for one actor to go on location). In the same film, a plane landing behind a sky-scraper in Hong Kong is also a digitally manipulated image.

In keeping with the adage, 'a lack of means is a means in itself', Nigerian producers are doubly creative in the way they trick the audience. In *Raging Storm* (a 1997 film directed by Tade Ogidan), there is a very powerful scene in which Francis Onwochei (both producer and lead actor in this case) is crushed by a lorry. Carefully researched, this extremely effective stunt was created not just by very astute cutting of the action, but also by using a dummy, flattened by a speeding articulated vehicle.

Yet, as the Nigerian video industry has expanded, the producers have moved beyond cheap stunts. Thanks to a television series produced over a number of years in collaboration with the Nigerian police, Tade Ogidan was able to get hold of weapons, uniforms and a helicopter for his film *Hostages*. In *Dangerous Twins* (Part II), his scene with a car accident is very realistically portrayed, and in *Osuofia in London* the limousine and the London mansion are not cardboard cut-outs. As to digitally manipulated images, these are also becoming less gratuitous in the way they are used and of better quality: in *Dangerous Twins*, Ramsey Nouah plays the role of twin brothers and in many of the scenes, both appear on the screen simultaneously using a special effect that even a professional would be at pains to detect.

Technical back-up (such as the camera crane, dolly and tracking rails) has become increasingly important in 'larger scale' productions, but this equipment is used more for impact than for the aesthetic of qualities of a shot. For example, it is used in 'The Making of ...' extra footage which sometimes introduces or accompanies the film on video. In 'The Making of *Oduduwa*' the crane and tracks are in full-view of the spectators and are clearly a matter of pride for the producer. Meanwhile the microphone is lacking even the most basic accessory of a wind-shield.

As well as this promotional aspect, using equipment such as a camera crane has much less to do with the production value of camera movements than the impression it makes during filming. Artistic success or the technical quality of the shot is secondary; the directors know that their films are only going to be shown, in most cases, on a very small screen. The aesthetic is less important than the emotional impact. What counts above all is that the scene is striking, emotional and effective. The principal objective is always the intensity of the narrative and the impact of the acting.

This obsession with impact is surely one of the keys to the success of Nigerian films, and is consistent with the analysis made by the Malian playwright Moussa Konate on the tastes of African audiences:

> Why do African audiences give such credit to American B movies and to Indian cinema? Firstly, the films that are watched across Africa are distinctive not for their depth or their individuality, on the contrary, the same themes are repeated from one film to the next; secondly, they are characterised by a certain old-fashioned sentimentality which is elaborated in the songs and dances. All in all, there is nothing there that would make you predict their success; a view that is shared by a number of African filmmakers, who still consider that cinema has to be serious to be rated. What American B movies and Indian cinema have in common is their capacity to make an emotional impact, and it is because they strike a chord that they appeal to the general public. A more educated audience would criticise them for all kinds of reasons, but they can't

deny that even though they might not like these films, they are rarely boring.[5]

Not only have Nigerian directors recreated the successful formulas of Indian and American models, they have also succeeded in supplanting them with the audiences. Indian cinema is still very popular in Northern Nigeria (where some picture houses still show 35mm Bollywood films), even if it has lost some ground in Kano where a local law, adopted after the establishment of Sharia, meant that a compulsory number of screenings were reserved each week for Hausa films. American films have fallen victim to cinema closures across the whole of the south of Nigeria. They still have a presence, thanks mainly to the pirated copies, but they form only a very limited part of the video market. The majority of consumers clearly prefer locally produced films.[6]

Nigeria is an industrial nation and it is also one of the main centres for forgery in Africa. Like many Asiatic countries which have built their economies by copying western designs, Nigeria uses the art of counterfeit in its video industry, including recycling the names of films: *Pretty Woman*, *Sharon Stone*, *Die Another Day*.[7] But the most striking example of imitation of a foreign model is Hausa musical theatre, transferred from the Indian film studios of Bollywood. The Hausa films even use the same commercial techniques. For example, in India the producers make more money sometimes from the film music, sold separately as an audio-cassette, than from the film itself. Such films are a huge success locally but are not taken very seriously anywhere else. Eddie Ugbomah, a filmmaker from Southern Nigeria, gives a damning portrait of Hausa films:

> These films that they are making are purely and simply Indian films. Singing for thirty minutes, dancing for the following thirty minutes. And that's it.[8]

In the French journal *Cinéastes*, Emmanuel Vincenot discussed the film *Khusufi 2*:

> In the dance numbers (apparently restricted to two or three per film), Hausa musicals give themselves the same freedoms as the Bollywood films on which they were modelled: continuities of space are interrupted for the duration of the song, the dancers can change their costumes at any time; so that only the melody provides a link between the shots. The artistic quality of these sequences doesn't come anywhere near the standards of perfection of the Bombay films, and even though the logistics of production are industrial, the actual conditions under which the films are directed are basic: the framing is hesitant, the lighting is poorly controlled and the dances are not always well timed. However, the energy of some of the

5. Moussa Konate, writer, publisher and organizer of the *Etonnants Voyageurs* festival in Bamako, which has an off-shoot in *Etonnants Scenarios* dedicated to the adaptation of literary works for cinema and television. The text cited here is an extract from the journal *Notre Librairie* (a review of literatures of the South), No. 149, *Cinemas d'Afrique*, October/December 2002.

6. The appearance on the Nigerian market of the South African company Nu Metro has changed the situation a bit since 2004, bringing back American movies to the cinemas and to the video-market.

7. A trilogy which launched the career of the diva Geneviève Nnaji – the third episode of this film was called *Sharon Stone in Abuja*.

8. Quoted from Okoh Aihie, *African Movie Directors in their Own Words* (National Film Institute, Jos, 2004).

dancers in performing the 'smurf' or the 'moonwalk' from the great era of 'Sydney' and 'Billie Jean', give the Nigerian films a kitsch feel which is a far cry from the languorous movements of the Hindu dancers. For all that, the directors continue to promote the elegance of their women: here as in Bombay, ugly people have no place except in their incarnations as negative characters (for example, the fickle or argumentative wife).[9]

Despite the mocking tone of this description it shouldn't be forgotten that this is an emerging film industry, aimed at a popular audience (for whom it represents a very important kind of freedom),[10] and in a region which has one of the highest levels of illiteracy in the world. For those who ridicule the eccentricities of Hausa video it would be interesting to see if they will have the same opinion in a few years time. Popular Indian cinema, which for a long time was mocked in the West, is no longer an object of ridicule. One of its biggest hits, *Devdas*, was premiered at the 2002 Cannes Film Festival. This film didn't rise from obscurity: it is the twelfth re-make of a 1917 Bengali novel.[11]

Nigerian films, which also proliferate through re-makes and multiple sequels, are improving all the time and will end up surprising their critics. The accumulation of films, whatever their quality, does have one advantage: it creates a visual and narrative culture. When they were young, many of the great creative talents of the developing world were soaking up the sights and sound of popular films.[12] Is it a coincidence that one of the great contemporary ambassadors of British Cinema is the Anglo-Indian director Gurinder Chadha (creator of *Bend it Like Beckham* and *Bride and Prejudice*)?[13]

Even if the critics haven't yet begun to take Nigerian video seriously, film distributors in Britain are already interested. In 2004 Obi Emelonye's *Echoes of War* was the first Nigerian film to be screened at four London cinemas that the British Board of Film Classification had just recently authorized to be fitted out for for video screenings.[14]

9. 'Haoullywood', article in *Cineastes*, February/March 2004.
10. See Chapter 4 on Hausa video and the Film Profile of *Khusufi I* on p.85.
11. See *Atlas du cinema*, published by Cahiers du cinema, April 2003.
12. In the publication *Memoire de cinephiles* (Cannes Film Festival, 2004), the sculptor Ousmane Sow recalls the screenings he saw as a child at the cinema in Dakar:
> Screenings sometimes lasted more than four hours, during which time some of the more inebriated of the audience danced and sang along with the Arabic music to a film which they had seen at least a dozen times. By the fourth film the projectionist would try to shorten the length of the session by taking out one or two reels, which provoked a slanging match between the audience and himself. We used to clap when acts of heroism were portrayed. I was so used to this that when I arrived in Paris in 1957, I was surprised and embarrassed to realise that the audience there was furious with me for clapping.
13. Born in Kenya to a family originally from the Punjab.
14. *Nollywood* supplement of *New Age*, 3 December 2004.

Film Profile No. 3
Hit the Street
Directed by Chico Ejiro

Date of release: 2004
Production/Distribution:
Infinity Merchants
Filmscript: Osita Okoli, based
on an idea by Chico Ejiro
Cast: Sandra Achums,
Abubakar Yakubu, Florence
Onuma, Victoria Inyama,
Benita Nzeribe, Jim Iyke & Elo
Ejeta

Chico Ejiro is said to be the most prolific of Nigerian directors, with more than a hundred films attributed to him. The prologue for *Hit the Street*, set in the present, creates the scenario of a murder (which you don't see) and then the suicide of one of its heroines, Juliet (sympathetically filmed). With the exception of the Epilogue, the film is a long flash-back. The film tells the story of three young women and a man who work in a bank in Lagos and are put under a lot of pressure by their department. They have to make money and attract important clients by whatever means, including selling themselves. Juliet is a principled woman but when her husband accuses her unjustly of neglecting the home and their only daughter, his criticisms cause her to rebel and take a decisive step: without any remorse she sleeps with her first client. After all, she is the one who keeps the family afloat; her unemployed husband just does odd jobs.

Tope, another young banker, plays the game without any qualms of conscience. Only Nneka, a devoted and puritanical evangelist, resists, and manages to escape being raped by one of her clients (this sequence is highly theatrical and not very credible, whereas other action/fight scenes are handled much better). Nneka also has to endure intense sexual harassment from her boss who puts her under a great deal of pressure and plays tricks on her.

As well as the three women, there is Chike, who takes a particular interest in looking after the clients (this role is played by the incredible Jim Iyke, dubbed the 'bad boy' of Nigerian home-videos). He gets brilliant results by sleeping with a wealthy business woman. Everything is going well until the day that Juliet introduces him to her daughter Aisha, who is much more elegant and sexy than her corpulent mother. This is a great scene which shows that Chico Ejiro's talent as a director is wasted on stringing together such low-grade productions.

As one might expect from the first frames, everything ends horribly: Juliet's daughter dies suddenly, just as her mother is in bed doing a deal with a client. Her husband comes looking for her and brings Aisha's body to his wife's hotel bedroom. In this scene, which offers a surreal display of bad taste, the father seems more troubled by having been cuckolded than by the death of his daughter. Just after this, Juliet learns that she has been laid off by the bank because a blood test has revealed she is HIV-positive.

Meanwhile, the sexually confident Tope is beaten by an 'area boy' hired by the jealous wife of a client. As to Nneka, she is arrested when her boss accuses her of having sold information to a business, when he himself has stolen the files.

Chike manages to get into the bed of the daughter of his voluminous client. A little while later the girl tells him that she is pregnant. Furious, he refuses to take responsibility and pushes the girl violently out of a car. Finally, Juliet, who has lost everything (her child, husband and job) takes herself to the bank, pushes her way into the director's office and shoots dead the two bosses who have destroyed her life. She then turns the gun on herself just as Nneka comes running into the room. The film ends with Nneka, alone at home, quoting in an interior monologue from the Bible: 'All is vanity'. A fitting summary after an hour and a half of horror and ignominy, portrayed in all its glory by Chico Ejiro, who doesn't shy away from excessive violence, vulgarity, or bad taste. The essential thing is to grab the audience by the throat from the opening shots, and then keep up the pace.

4 Selling Like Hot Cake: Box Office & Statistics
Pierre Barrot

◀◀

According to Tunde Oladunjoye (see his chapter, pp. 62–9) 'It is easier to extract water from a stone than to get reliable statistics of the home video industry in Nigeria.' This is as true of profits as it is of sales figures, however, for the quantity and nature of the films produced there is an undisputed source of statistical information in the National Film and Video Censors Board (NFVCB). The one limitation to the data is that they only relate to films that are legally distributed. The black market for films goes on to one side, and nobody can quite assess the scale of it, so the figures are approximate.

The NFVCB was created in 1993. It was fully functioning from June 1994, two years after the 'home-video' industry got started with the release of *Living in Bondage* (1992). Initially based in Lagos, the Board opened other offices in Abuja, Kano and Onitsha (the second most important market after Idumota).

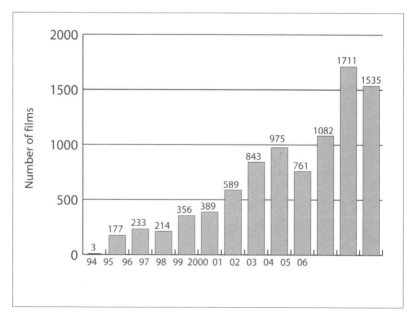

Figure 1 Number of films rated by the National Film & Video Censors Board, 1994–2006
Source: National Film and Video Censors Board, 2007

Table 1   Number of films made in English, Hausa, Yoruba & other languages

Language	1994/2001	2002/2006	2006	Total for 1994–2006
English	1067 (38%)	3259 (54%)	641 (42%)	4326 (49%)
Yoruba	1041 (37%)	1709 (28%)	563 (37%)	2750 (31%)
Hausa	633 (22%)	984 (16%)	279 (18%)	1617 (18%)
Others	63 (2%)	112 (2%)	52 (3%)	175 (2%)
Total	2804	6064	1535	8868

Source: National Film and Video Censors Board, 2007

In ten years the number of films endorsed by the Board multiplied sevenfold. The total since 2004 is the equivalent of between three and five new films each working day. The decline in the number of films in 2002 can be explained by a moratorium on the release of films ordered by the marketers' association to prevent a glut in the market.

Even though a large number of producers and distributors are Igbo,[1] the proportion of films made in the Igbo language is relatively small. The trail-blazing film *Living in Bondage*, however, was shot in Igbo and sold 200,000 copies, providing a great impetus to the field of production.

But today, Igbo distributors prefer films made in English, possibly because this gives them access to a wider nationwide market. On the other hand, a fair number of Yoruba producers shoot their films in their own language and reach an audience mainly in the south-west of the country (as well as neighbouring Benin). There is also an increase in the films made in the Edo language of the Benin City region (50 films in 2006). As can be seen in Table 2, the proportion of films being made in Hausa has slightly decreased. Having outstripped the number of Yoruba films made between 1999 and 2001, Hausa films have been left behind. One reason could be the instigation of Sharia law in 2000 and the restrictions that this brought into a dozen northern states. This is particularly true in Kano, the hub of the Hausa video industry, where as well as the Federal Censors Board, a State censoring office operates with even more rigorous moral criteria.

Table 2   Estimated turnover of the video industry (in Naira), 1994–2006

1994 (1)	1999 (1)	2000 (1)	2003 (2)	2006 (1)
250 million	3.4 billion	6.45 billion	12 billion	20 billion

Sources: (1) NFVCB; (2) Interview in *Tell* magazine given by Rosalyn Odeh, former Director of the NFVCB.

In 2006, 20 billion Naira were equivalent to US$ 160 million. Applying these figures to the 1,535 films registered that year, it works out at an average of US$ 104,000 per film, and corresponds to

1. The Igbo people (originally from South-East of Nigeria, for a time known as Biafra) are Nigeria's third largest ethnic group. They are particularly active in business and control a significant part of the video trade. The town of Onitsha is the second biggest market for buying and selling films in the country.

approximately 37,000 V-CDs sold of each film. (The distribution of VHS tapes had almost ceased by 2006, especially in the South of the country.) Seeing as the industry's revenue is linked directly to the video market[2] it is possible that the total turnover has been over-estimated by the NFVCB.

In a presentation at the Forum for New Cinema in Berlin in 2004, the actor-producer Francis Onwochei,[3] gave the following statistics: 1,200 films released into the market each year, with a production cost of less than US$ 21,000[4] and an average sale of 50,000 copies per film, which is the equivalent to a total turnover of US$ 150 million. Such figures are even more surprising than those of the NFVCB: even if the costs of reproduction and marketing the films are exaggerated, the lack of proportion between the cost of production given (US$ 21,000 per film) and the revenue (US$ 130,000) seems excessive.

In the same year, the Minister for Information and National Planning gave the following figures: 30 billion Naira (equivalent to US$ 230 million at 2004 exchange rates) to produce a total of 6,000 films since the Nigerian video industry kicked off. These figures suggest an average income of less than US$ 40,000 per film. This is of course an average figure for a period of over ten years, but the difference between these figures and the estimates made by the NFVCB (US$ 104,000 in 2004) and those of Francis Onwochei (US$ 130,000) is striking. Oladunjoye's point about the difficulty of getting reliable statistics is clearly apt.

There is no regulated 'Box office' in Nigeria and it is quite rare for distributors to publish credible sales figures. According to Jenzeri Zakari Okwori,[5] in the early days of the video industry, Amaka Igwe's *Rattlesnake II*, would have sold 50,000 copies during its first month of sales. Ten years later, Tunde Kelani reported sales of between 100,000 and 120,000 of *Agogo Eewo*. The Hausa film *Wassila*, directed by Yakubu Lere, reputedly sold more than 100,000 copies. *Buri*, another Hausa film, produced by Hamisu Lamido Iyan-Tama, sold 70,000 copies.

It was rare to learn of significantly higher sales figures than these except for the 400,000 claimed in 2004 for Kingsley Ogoro's *Osuofia in London*.[6] This director, at the time of the launch of his subsequent film *Across the Niger*, claimed to have spent 30 million Naira (US$235,000) on this 'large-scale production'. In the Nigerian context, he would have had to sell at least 150,000 to 250,000 copies to get a return on such a large investment in the video market. This is the reason that Kingsley Ogoro has turned his attention to selling films for cinema screenings, especially at the more prestigious venues with higher ticket prices.

Almost all of the sales figures cited for the video market are estimates. Conflicts between producers and the distributors ('marketers') are both frequent and legendary. There are cases of distributors being cheated by their producers (see Don Pedro Obaseki's observations on

2. Sales to television accounts for only a small proportion of revenue, the most regular client being the commercial channel Africa Magic which pays as little as US$ 700 per film.
3. Former Secretary-general of the Independent Television Producers Association of Nigeria (ITPAN).
4. According to Tunde Kelani, the most professional of Nigerian film directors: 'To make a decent film, I couldn't budget for less than 7 million Naira (US$ 50,000).' (*Saturday Punch*, 10 January 2004).
5. Professor in the Department of English and Drama of Ahmadu Bello University, Zaria), and author of the paper 'A dramatized society: representing rituals of human sacrifice as efficacious in Nigerian home-video-movies'. in *Journal of African Cultural Studies*, Volume 16, Issue 1 June 2003, pp.7–23.
6. This figure was given by Francis Onwochei in the *Nollywood* supplement of *New Age*, May 2004.

Table 3   The increasing severity of the Board of Censors, 1994–2006

	1994–2001	2002–2006
Films unsuitable for under-18s	736 (out of 2,804)	5,227 (out of 6,064)
Expressed as percentage	26%	86%
Children's films	1	1

Table 4   The video industry as a creator of employment

Nigerian states	Video distributors (Officially recorded)
Abia	129
Abuja	201
Adamawa	3
Akwa-Ibom	5
Anambra	226
Bauchi	2
Benue	3
Borno	6
Cross River	2
Delta	17
Ebonyi	1
Edo	375
Enugu	115
Imo	91
Kaduna	16
Kano	181
Kebbi	3
Kogi	1
Kwara	210
Lagos	98
Nassarawa	12
Niger	38
Ogun	8
Ondo/Ekiti	301
Osun	265
Oyo	65
Plateau	3
Rivers	204
TOTAL	2581

Bus used by retailers in Ikoyi, Lagos, to promote the latest V-CD releases from Gold Pictures film company, 2007

(© Robert Minangoy)

p. 75), but often distributors are accused of running off with all the takings or of cooking the books. After the sale of the first 20,000 copies of his film *Ileke*, Greg Odutayo, received no further money from his distributor. He ended up taking him to court and the man was imprisoned. Tunde Kelani also had cause to part ways from his distributor and had to delay the release of this film *The Campus* Queen (it was finally released in March 2004 and only put out on video the following year).

The figures in Table 3 (p. 35) indicate a radical political change on the part of the Censors Board. The proportion of films passed as suitable for minors has been cut by a fifth. Such a spectacular development can only be explained by a change in the leadership of an institution. The period characterized by such strict standards was under the leadership of Rosalyn Odeh who took over from Ademola James in June 2001. In particular, the Board endeavoured to discourage films about witchcraft under her guidance. Table 3 also shows the near complete absence of

Retailers in Ikoyi, Lagos, promoting some of the 50 or so new releases per month from Gold Pictures, 2007

(© Robert Minangoy)

films for children, and one can easily imagine the influence that the NFVCB itself might have on the production of such films. When a producer sees that younger viewers will have few opportunities to watch a film given a 'suitable for children' classification, he is unlikely to invest in something so unlikely to succeed. The film *Baby Police*, for example, was classified as unsuitable for under-18s by the NFVCB, even though it was clearly aimed at a young audience. It is a comedy in which the leading character is a dwarf playing the role of a junior policeman, and it is neither violent nor risqué in content. But the '18' classification, imposed by Rosalyn Odeh, matched with a restriction, preventing it being screened on television, could simply be put down to the use of 'slang and vulgar expressions'. This criterion was in fact ranked by the NFVCB's report in their *Film and Video Directory*, 2004, as the 'problem' that caused most offence; far ahead of 'indecency' (which was ranked in 7th place) and 'excessive violence' (which was only ranked 9th).

Pierre Barrot

The inventory carried out by the NFVCB of video outlets (see Table 4, p. 35), is extremely patchy: a large number of the people working in video rental and re-sale in the built-up areas of Lagos do not appear at all; a realistic assessment of the number of active video-clubs in the nation as a whole is thought to be 23,000. However, these figures show the impact and the extent of the video phenomenon across the whole country.

It is estimated that the video-industry employs in the region of 200,000 people, most of whom are involved in the video trade rather than in their production.

Table 5 The domination of video-viewing

Population having access to a video player at home	34 million
Percentage of the urban population with video player	65%

Source: Study carried out by Gallup-Nigeria for Canal-France International (May 2003)

VHS video cassettes (which sell for 250 Naira each) are still used in Northern Nigeria and are more affordable than V-CDs (350 Naira each). The latter have become more popular in the South of the country as the sound and image quality is superior and V-CD players are less expensive. DVD technology, by contrast is still only used by a wealthier minority.

As with the production side, distribution in the Nigerian market remains informal and decentralized; it depends for the most part on a multitude of small, specialized booths or video-stalls. In 2005, the South African company Nu Metro tried something new by opening a vast, top of the range *Media Store* in Lagos and by testing out film sales at petrol stations. Another newcomer to the market, Dove Media.[7] successfully experimented with selling videos during their 'crusades' and other religious events.

Don Pedro Obaseki, one of the heavyweights of the Nigerian video business, launched a mobile distribution system at the end of 2006. He set up 50 kiosks which served as warehouses for 70 distributors on motorbikes who dashed through the neighbourhoods selling films in the street as well as delivering to people's houses. The motorbikes were kitted out with a screen and a video player so that the customers could check the quality of what they were buying. In January 2007, Don Pedro declared that his sales target was 25,000 copies per day.[8]

Currently, the other revolution in Nigerian distribution is selling on the internet. This mode of sale hardly affects the local market at all as electronic methods of payment hardly exist. Selling on line relates essentially to the overseas market and most notably to the African diasporas of Europe and North America. Hundreds of films can be

7. Linked to the powerful Redeemed Christian Church, one of the most important evangelical churches in Nigeria.
8. Source: businessdayonline.com, 5 January 2007.
9. Among the on-line sales sites active in 2007: nigeriamovies.net (selling in DVD format, although others offer different formats); africanmoviesdirect.com; allafricanmovies.com; nigeriafilms.com; izognmovies.com; and jjjnigermovies.com.

ordered through the increasing number of websites,[9] which also attract a growing number of hits from people curious about the industry. The introduction of some of these people to Nigerian video has provoked vigorous debates in the many discussion groups set up on commercial sites or on those promoting Nollywood.[10] Some consumers from Western countries are astonished to discover the poor quality (both technical and artistic) of the majority of the films. It contrasts dramatically with some of the professional and attractive-looking outlets that exist online. In fact, one characteristic of the Nollywood industry is its tendency to invest far more in marketing than in the product itself. It is impossible to put a figure to the number of films sold via the internet, but some distributors seem to rely heavily on this method. A single V-CD is sold for about US$ 4 on the internet, whereas its price on the Nigerian market would rarely be more than US$ 2.5.

Table 6 The stars and their fees

Top stars	Record fees in $US
Geneviève Nnaji	23,000
Chinedu Ikedieze	8,000
Nkem Owoh	7,800
Emeka Ike	6,600

Source: *New Age*, May 2004 and nigeriamovies.net, 2006

Whereas producers' incomes and distributors' sales figures are still completely obscure, the money earned by the stars is increasingly in the public domain. In May 2004, the *Nollywood* supplement of the paper *New Age*, dedicated a whole section to the salaries of the 11 most sought-after Nigerian actors.[11] The terms 'Big Five', for the actresses, and 'Big Six' for the actors were used for the first time. The article reported that Nkem Owoh earned one million Naira (US$ 7,800) for each of the two parts of *Osuofia in London*. Similarly, the actress Omotola Jalade-Ekeinde considered a million Naira to be the benchmark, refusing any role offered for less. Furthermore, Geneviève Nnaji's fees had risen to three million Naira (US$ 23,000) by 2004.[12] *New Age*[13] revealed that by starring in 12 films for an average fee of two million Naira, Geneviève Nnaji had been able to earn as much as 24 million Naira (US$ 187,000) in 2004 alone.

The producer-distributors see themselves as victims of a bidding system linked to a celebrity culture which they themselves created. In October 2004 they ordered a total boycott of the most highly paid and capricious actors. Added to the list of boycotted actors was one director also considered to be too demanding: Tchidi Chikere, creator of a number of box-office hits including *Blood Sisters* and *Under Fire*.

According to the producer Eddie Ugbomah, 'these monsters were

10. Some on-line sales sites include discussion fora. Such fora are also found on at least a dozen of the websites of Nollywood stars: Geneviève Nnaji's site, which was one of the first to be put on the web by a Nollywood actor, was no longer functioning by the start of 2007.

11. This group comprised: Geneviève Nnaji, Stephanie Okereke, Omotola Jalade-Ekeinde, Rita Dominic, Stella Damasus Aboderin, of the female, and Nkem Owoh, Ramsey Nouah, Richard Mofe-Damijo, Jim Iyke, Emeka Ike, Desmond Eliott, of the male stars. The nigeriamovies.net website has information on 150 home-video actors and directors.

12. In the making of a Nigerian film, the amount of time that an actor has to spend on set shooting is rarely more than two weeks.

13. 8 October 2004.

Pierre Barrot

Clarion Chukwura Abiola, one of Nollywood's superstars. Almost half of the total budget for the films is set aside for actors' fees (© Robert Minangoy)

created by the distributors.' The latter clearly think they have the power of life or death over their creations. One might assume that the 'monsters' no longer depend on the sorcerer-apprentices who created them, given the quasi-godlike status accorded them by their adoring public. However, the Nigerian distributors demonstrated their power throughout 2004 by maintaining their boycott of the highest paid actors. While they were sidelined, some of the banished tried their luck beyond Nollywood (Geneviève Nnaji, for example, as an R&B singer and a beauty consultant), or as an actor outside of the Nollywood circuit (Stephanie Okereke shot films with the South African channel M-Net). Yet all of them went back into shooting Nollywood films at the end of their year in the wilderness. Only Geneviève Nnaji held out for a little longer against the producers who had snubbed her, but by 2007 she was back on the video covers. Nollywood is an addiction that can't easily be shaken off, by the audiences or by the actors.

Film Profile No. 4
Dangerous Twins (Parts I, II and III)
Directed by Tade Ogidan

Tayie is a businessman based in London. He lives happily with his English wife Judy but he has not been able to have children. During an unexpected trip to Nigeria he confides in his twin brother Kehinde, worrying that he might be sterile. His brother (also a businessman), agrees to swap places with Taiye in London just long enough to get Judy pregnant. Taiye meanwhile replaces him both as head of his small business and head of his family, his wife and three children. Neither wife discovers the trick that has been played on them, even though both twins are behaving unusually. Taiye, who has become a bit too 'British' has great difficulty in adapting to the very particular rules of the game that exist in Nigeria. By contrast, Kehinde relaxes into London life. Not only does Judy get pregnant but Taiye's business venture prospers: Kehinde, having introduced a system of back-handers, signs deal after deal. There is no longer any chance that he will want to return to Lagos to take up his old life. The descent into hell begins for Taiye...

Dangerous Twins is a surprising film. It is rare to see such a switch from light drama to horror. One scene (suggested but not filmed), of the children's murder, introduces a bitter edge. Some aspects of Nigerian life-style, seen from the perspective of London, may look comic, but some of the realities of the country are also portrayed. Tade Ogidan was criticized for the shocking scene in which the children are executed by armed bandits while their father runs away under the pretext of fetching help. He justified his decision by saying that the scene was not gratuitous, and because he understood the extent of criminality in his country, having worked closely with the Nigerian police on a television series.

What stays with you after watching *Dangerous Twins* is the accomplished performance of Ramsey Nouah, whose career took off after this film. Tade Ogidan stands out from other Nigerian directors for his skill with the actors. *Dangerous Twins* is practically a test case for this in the direction of the same actor in a spectrum of roles: twins who each have in turn to play the character of the other. One of them, a smooth talker and liar, is the catalyst for a series of complicated situations. Ramsey

Date of Release: 2004
Production: OGD Pictures.
Filmscript: Niji Akanni & Tade Ogidan
Cast: Ramsey Nouah, Stella Damasus Aboderin, Danielle Mubarak, Lanre Balogun & Bimbo Akintola
Cinematography: Jonathan Gbemuotor.
Dialogue in English

*Ramsey Nouah, one of the most
sought-after Nollywood actors,
during the filming of Tade Ogidan's*
Dangerous Twins
(© Jean-Claude Moschetti/REA)

Nouah is at times a wide-boy (not the most challenging part), and at times very serious, which makes him even more convincing. Similarly, Lanre Balogun's role is very demanding when he becomes impassive; his icy expression when faced with Tayie's demands for money is more terrifying than the murder scene that follows.

An equally impressive scene in terms of the interiorisation of the acting occurs in Tade Ogidan's earlier film *Saving Alero*: the character portrayed by Francis Onwochie, is slapped by his wife, and reacts with an anger that is chill, silent and contained – more powerful than any of the verbal fireworks with which most Nollywood audiences are fed.

5 Audacity, Scandal & Censorship
Pierre Barrot

◀◀◀

If Nigerian films were only popular in Nigeria then the phenomenon could be put down to a particular local fascination, something larger than life from a country that is larger than life. But the films have been an impressive success right across Africa. They are found on video-cassette or on V-CD in the markets of nearly all anglophone countries. About one million films (VHS or V-CD) are distributed every year in Kenya[1] and hardly a day passes when there isn't a Nigerian film on one of its television channels. In Ghana, the almost daily broadcasting of these films across the four local channels has resulted in a new protectionist law (Film and Development Classification Bill). The demand for Nigerian films even led M-Net to launch a new channel in December 2003 called Africa Magic, because the pan-African DSTV satellite output suffered from being too South African in its image. The programming for the new station is 80 per cent Nigerian films. In 2006 a second channel in the same arena was launched by the British company, Zenithfilms, on Rupert Murdoch's BSkyB network.[2] Several Nigerian directors have been invited to make films in Sierra Leone[3] and in Benin.[4] Many others are filming in Ghana and Cameroon on independent productions.

Journalist and writer Helen Muchimba describes the impact of Nigerian films in Zambia:

> The stories tend to be quite simple but very dramatic and heavy on the emotions: the women wail and are avaricious money lovers; the men are just as emotional and very vengeful...Throw in a gibbering bone-rattling juju man and Bible-waving preacher and what you have is a brew of conflict, revenge, trials and tribulations – the likes of which are keeping most Zambians, especially in the capital city, Lusaka, glued to TV screens for hours on end... The mother of one family complained that 'the children had started talking like Nigerians. You hear them say yes-o and no-o, and at every possible opportunity they say "God forbid!".[5]

This success isn't restricted to anglophone Africa. Nigerian films are broadcast on television (without any sub-titles) in at least seven

1. See the chapter by Ogova Ondego (pp. 114–18).
2. Source: Elisabeth Lequeret, Radio France Internationale's website 20 August 2006.
3. Fred Amata made *Bai Bureh Goes to War*, with Geneviève Nnaji, in this way.
4. Tunde Kelani was brought in to shoot several films at the request of beninois production company Laha.
5. Cited from an article in *BBC – Focus on Africa*, October–December 2004.

Pierre Barrot

6. In 2004, not only were Hubert Ogunde's 35mm films (rarely shown in Nigeria) continuing to be screened at the Cine Concorde, the largest cinema in Cotonou, but the independent cinema Okpe Oluwa specialised in screening Nigerian videos.

7. Film directed by Tunde Hundeyin which came out in 1995 (followed by a sequel in 2001). Tunde Hundeyin is a filmmaker who went back to video after working in film in the 1980s.

8. In March 2004, only four Ghanaian films were monitored by the Ghanaian Board of Censors compared to 18 Nigerian films. According to the director Socrate Safo, the number of registered Ghanaian producers went from 47 at the end of the 1990s to just seven in 2004. And in the same year, out of 26 officially active distributors, 18 were Nigerian.

9. Even though religious issues are seen as potentially explosive in Nigeria, they are still included in the films. Preacher Mike Bamiloye has specialised in making 'evangelical' films. The drug addict in Fred Amata's *The Addict* is helped through detox by a pastor. In Chico Ejiro's *Festival of Fire*, it is Catholics who make a stand against infanticide and ritual crimes in a fetishist village. There is even a Hausa film which denounces corrupt marabouts, but its distribution was blocked, not by the censors, but by the distributors themselves, who feared reprisals from the same marabouts.

10. Since the re-establishment of democracy in Nigeria in 1999, disturbances between Christians and Muslims have led to thousands of deaths. Of all the confrontations that occurred, the one in Kaduna in November 2002 caused an international stir, provoking the shift of the Miss Universe election from Abuja to London. The riot was caused by an article that appeared in the press saying that the Prophet himself wouldn't have been insensible to the beauty of the contestants.

francophone countries: Niger, Cameroon, the Democratic Republic of Congo, Benin, Togo, Senegal and even Burkina Faso. In Benin, Yoruba films are a big hit, not just in video-clubs but also in cinemas.[6]

In Côte d'Ivoire, political unrest unsettled the market, but before the rebel offensive in 2002, the journalist Jahman Anikulapo described his encounter with the video traders in Adjamé, Abidjan. According to his guide, Ramon:

> They sell mostly Nigerian films and a few from Ghana...Pete Edochie, Liz Benson, Richard Mofe-Damijo, Bimbo Akintola...they are all very popular here. 'How's business?': the question was asked of one wide boy, the video seller. 'Business is booming. We have sold 10,000 copies of *Iyawo Alhaji*[7] and *Blood Money* sold 8,000 copies. We've run out of stock.

In Ghana the competition from Nigeria has been damaging to local video production which began in the 1980s, and through the 1990s was respected for its dynamism.[8] Today, Ghanaian audiences find their own home grown films too patchy, weak in storylines, or too serious to be watchable.

The Nigerian video industry got started a bit later than Ghana's but developed at a much faster pace. Audiences are always stunned, experiencing a whole gamut of sensations.[9] Regarded as 'beyond taboo', Nigerian films roll out crime, drugs, prostitution, witchcraft, adultery, corruption, politics and even religion. Almost anything goes.

Hollywood accustomed people to revisiting, for example, the assassination of John Kennedy, but in most African countries the idea of a dramatized version of a coup d'etat is unimaginable, in the interests of national security. Nigerian filmmakers have even broken this taboo: in *The President Must Not Die*, Zeb Ejiro took his own head of state hostage, and before this Teco Benson, in *State of Emergency*, liquidated half of the government. Amaka Igwe, in his 2004 film *Apostle Kasali*, dramatized the story of a young innocent born into a Muslim family but seized by a vocation to be an evangelist preacher and miracle-maker.

Nigerian directors are not afraid to broach any subject, no matter how sensitive. They even manage to use religion to make people laugh, in a country where fanaticism and inter-denominational confrontations are rife.[10] Thus video is ahead of society itself and perhaps can even foster its progress towards tolerance.

The freedoms expressed through Nigerian video production are exceptional in the African context. Despite the democratization of the 1990s, one is still struck by the amount of political and social control, and the level of moral conservatism. Freedom of expression is restricted both by tradition and by the recent inroads made by Islam and Evangelism. In order to stifle any regional expression or any evocation of

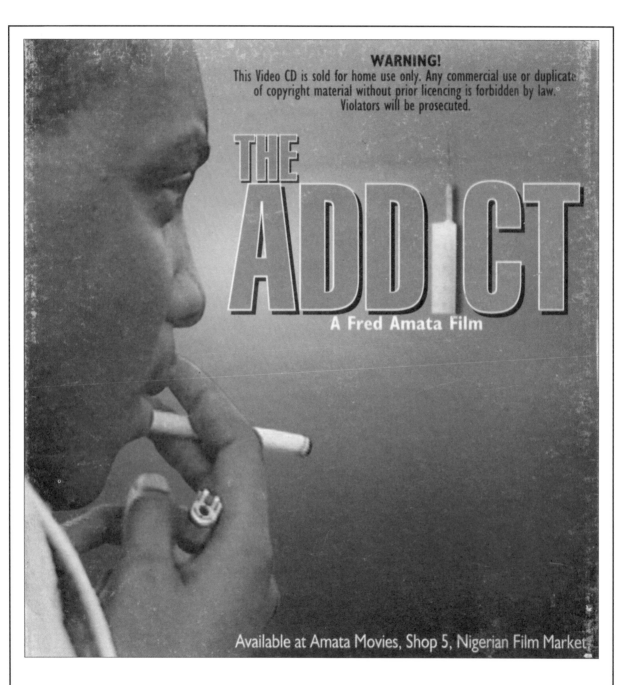

THE ADDICT

A Fred Amata Film

Available at Amata Movies, Shop 5, Nigerian Film Market

V-CD cover for Fred Amata's *The Addict*

ethnic tension, politicians raise the spectre of Rwanda and its 'Radio-Television Libre des Mille Collines'.[11] Once this fear is spread wide, it has an intimidating effect. People forget that the 'free' radio in question never represented freedom of expression. On the contrary, it was a propaganda instrument in the hands of a despotic regime capable of manipulating its captive audience, by denying access to any other source of news.

Although video production in Nigeria emerged during the era of military dictatorship,[12] it is one of the most impressive signs of freedom of expression in Africa. It is not surprising that this freedom of expression blossomed in both fiction writing and in a very specific field such as video. With fiction, people can say things that a journalist would find more difficult to say. 'Violence in Nigeria makes it one of the most dangerous areas in Africa for journalists', wrote *Reporters without Frontiers* in November 2004, adding that since the beginning of that year, it had recorded 72 cases where press freedom was at risk. For instance, in December 2006, Godwin Agbroko, one of the country's most famous journalists from the paper *This Day*, was shot in the neck as the presidential elections (often a murderous time) were getting underway.

Even though censorship is less severe since the re-establishment of democracy in Nigeria, there are still other ways of putting pressure on the media. In 2003, there was a cover story for *Tell* magazine that implicated close relatives of the Vice-President in a case of corruption. The issue was seized in a very particular manner; all the copies printed were compulsorily purchased as they left the print works. On the other hand, the country's leaders rarely take offence publicly at the way the political class is portrayed in the films. In Tunde Kelani's *Campus Queen*, the military governor (under a cloak of civility that makes him both likeable and credible) is in fact sensual, corrupt and murderous. By portraying so-called imaginary characters, fiction films do not provoke a reaction from the individuals who are targeted. For them protest would be seen as an admission of guilt.

The degree of freedom achieved by Nigerian films and the audacity shown by the producers is a result of the method of broadcasting. Most are never screened publicly, many are never shown on television. Destined for home consumption, they can side-step the rules that burden other media. In fact, for such films the only regulatory authority that counts is the actual consumer, who is free to buy or not, free to show the film to whoever he/she chooses in the privacy or 'free-zone' of home. Domestic video does not engender the same kind of public debate nor does it raise the same issues of social responsibility as television or the press.

Of course, the National Film and Video Censors Board (NFVCB) keeps a beady eye on content, and since 2001, has become more strict, with the proportion of films that are forbidden to under-18s rising

11. These broadcasts are considered to have been an important weapon in the 1994 genocide.

12. The year when the Nigerian home-video was born, 1992, is also the year that witnessed the fall of General Babangida's dictatorship. The major events of the year were a hunger riot and fraudulent, violent governorship elections. The following year, President Babangida organized a presidential election that was said to be free and fair. He later annulled the results; which led to chaos and Sani Abacha's fierce dictatorship. (See Marc-Antoine de Montclos, *Le Nigeria*, Karthala/IFRA, Paris, 1994).

from 36 to 92 per cent. At the same time, viewing restrictions for minors have also been applied to television broadcasts, something that was not done systematically in the past.[13]

Politics of this kind seems to have had a perverse effect: by attempting to prevent the television broadcasting of most of the films, the Censors Board has also made producers avoid developing a strategy specifically for this kind of broadcasting. Of course, most of their profits come from the domestic video market, but some producers, such as Tunde Kelani would like to see their work on television so that once the film has broken even financially, their message can reach the greatest number of people.

Kelani's films *Saworoide* and *Thunderbolt*, released in 1999 and 2000 respectively, were both given the 'general audience' classification (even though the first has a political assassination sequence, and the second includes a suggestion of a sexual encounter). At the time the NFVCB was led by Ademola James. When he was replaced by Rosalyn Odeh, Kelani's subsequent two films were classified '18' and denied

Nudity is the only taboo; actors on the set of a film directed by Theodore Anyanji

(© Jean-Claude Moschetti/REA)

13. In practice, television companies, which have to adhere to certain quotas for local production and who have to answer to their own regulatory authority, the National Broadcasting Commission (NBC), do not keep to the broadcasting prohibitions set by the Censorship Board for films. Films classified as '18' can be seen on private channels as well as on the federal public television network the Nigerian Television Authority (NTA). The NBC does not seem to want to sanction what are in effect illegal broadcasts.

broadcasting rights for television, even though their content was similar to, or even more anodyne than the earlier films.

In fact, what is worrying is that by giving nearly everything the classification 'NTBB' (not to be broadcast on television) it has made the producers irresponsible. They no longer have any reason to question the impact of their films, or to judge whether, for example, a particularly violent scene might be disturbing for children. It is of little importance as they haven't been given a 'suitable for children' classification, so that it is left up to parents to take the necessary precautions. As a result, video producers have been able to wash their hands of the issue. Moreover, they are covered by the NFVCB. In the belief that it has acted in everyone's best interests, it has in fact disincentivized producers. They might have considered the regulations for television broadcasting but there is no need.

As the product is restricted to the video market, it is the consumer who decides whether they are what they want. Besides, on television (the most passive of all forms of taking in images) you may watch a film that you don't want to see, while buying a video provides a degree of choice. It is up to the consumer alone to take responsibility.

Everywhere in the world there is a notable difference between what is produced for television and what is produced for the cinema: television productions tend to be more formulaic, conceived with a particular target audience in mind, for specific scheduled slots, often to very constraining specifications. Public service broadcasting has its standards and the private companies fall in with this as they are under pressure from viewing figures and advertisers. In many African countries, political pressure is the one that dominates all other constraints. By offering 'consensual' or 'federal' programming, television becomes dull. 'Our channels are boring', one officer admitted in the Office for National Culture in Kano. 'This is the reason for the success of home video.'

If people are bored with television (not only in Africa), then by contrast going to the cinema is liberating: a voluntary, active step. Faced with the big screen, the spectator's freedom of choice has just one limitation – not being allowed to interrupt the screening. Of course, this *is* a possibility for those watching videos at home. In Nigeria most production is aimed at this kind of 'narrow-casting', and its very particular context gives a great deal of freedom (and a minimum of responsibility) to both scriptwriters and producers. Apart from nudity, everything else is allowed: murder, suicide, torture, rape, incest and infanticide.

In Chico Ejiro's *Festival of Fire*, a fetishist disembowels babies with a kitchen knife. *Dangerous Twins* has a scene of child murder. The hero of *Raging Storm*, also by Tade Ogidan, following a pact with a fetishist/ satanic cult, has to sleep with his own daughter as 'payback' for the social success bestowed on him; he makes several suicide attempts to try to escape his fate. Although classed suitable for the 'general public', *The Mourning After* depicts a hanging. The hero of *Heritage* is tortured with electricity. In Chico Ejiro's *Hit the Street*, the body of a dead child is presented to its mother at the very moment that she is unfaithful to her husband. Films like *State of Emergency* are piled with corpses. In *Jealous Lovers*, a heroine addict injects himself in front of the camera, then tries to rape a woman (played by Geneviève Nnaji). The drug addict in *The Addict* stabs his mother in the stomach with a broken bottle. Geneviève Nnaji, once again seen in the film *Blood Sisters*, torments her own sister and ends up poisoning her. In *Legal War*, an armed bandit shoots a couple, then tries to shoot their baby but he has run out of bullets... The list of horrors seems endless, and yet the films cited here are not the worst.

If violence is omnipresent then sex is fairly rare,[14] or at least prudishly portrayed. There is no shortage of sexy actresses and scandals in Nigerian films, but nipples are never shown on screen. The two puritanical movements of Evangelism and Islam are united in their rejection of any female nudity. Rosalyn Odeh,[15] former director of the NFVCB rejoices in this:

> Until we have evidence to the contrary we can say that all the pornographic films distributed in Nigeria are pirated copies of foreign films and don't originate from Nigerian filmmakers.[16]

The fact that the only taboo respected in Nigerian films is nudity, seems to be appreciated in other African countries: 'In contrast to many western films, Nigerian video doesn't include embarrassing love scenes. In this way they respect the Kenyan view of Africans, or of what Africans should be', writes the Kenyan journalist Ogova Ondego.[17]

However, this point of view seems to be more representative of anglophone Africa (bound by Anglo-Saxon puritanism) than of francophone countries. In 2003, in Cameroon, when *Le Silence de la Forêt* (directed by the Cameroonian Bassek Ba Khobio) was shown, along with *Les Couilles de l'éléphant* (directed by Henri-Joseph Koumba Bididi), representatives from Kenya, Uganda, Nigeria and Ghana were unanimous in their judgement that the love scenes and nudity portrayed in both films were unsuitable for viewing in their own countries.

In reality, the restrictions imposed by the NFVCB, for sex, as for violence, can raise questions about hypocrisy. As to morality, you can show the worst kind of depravity, as long as you don't name it (for example, the NFVCB under the leadership of Rosalyn Odeh insisted that Tunde Kelani cut the word *ashawo*, meaning prostitute, from *Campus Queen*), Of course, neither buttocks nor breasts can be shown, but the most extreme violence is tolerated completely, provided that

14. 'Make war, not love' could be the motto of the Nigerian video industry.
15. Replaced in 2005 by Emeka Mba.
16. Preface of the *Film and Video Directory of Nigeria*, Volume 2, 2004 (Published by NFVCB, Lagos)
17. See chapter by Ogova Ondego, pp. 114–17.

Pierre Barrot

18. The expression 'Cachez ce sein que je ne saurais voir' [Hide this breast that I cannot see], is spoken by Tartuffe, one of Molière's characters, and has given the word tartufferie (hypocrisy) to the French language. Succeeding Rosalyn Odeh as head of the Board of Censors, Emeka Mba has applied less stringent classifications, and most importantly, has ended the connection between the 'under 18' classification and the prohibition from television broadcasting.

blood doesn't actually flow. At the premiere of Dangerous Twins, one journalist was astonished to see not a single drop of blood on the bodies of the dead children during the murder scene (previously described). 'The Board of Censors doesn't like it', was the substance of the director Tade Ogidan's reply. Hide this blood that I cannot see.[18]

Film Profile No. 5
The President Must Not Die
Directed by Zeb Ejiro

The President Must Not Die is an American style B-movie with a Nigerian flavour. The battle between the Board of Censors and Zeb Ejiro lasted for six months before the film was authorised for release with a new title. The intended title *The President Must Die*, was not politically correct in a country where about half of the heads of state since independence had died with different degrees of violence, before the end of their term of office.[1]

The film tells the story of a President of Nigeria who is kidnapped as he leaves a conference by a person posing as a bodyguard and armed with a belt of explosives. The kidnapper takes his captive to a disused factory, helped by accomplices, one of whom is a kind of 'Barbie doll' with light-coloured hair and a sizeable cleavage adorned with a large crucifix.

The President has a ransom on his head of US$ 60 million (quite a modest sum when compared to the US$ 3.5 billion siphoned off into western banks by the Sani Abacha regime). However, his entourage refuse to give in to blackmail. The President is finally released, at the end of a desperate fight, by a group of young, sexy, women warriors, who use their skills and grace in karate to great effect (their small feet are used on several occasions to crack the vertebrae of the villains as they lie on the floor).

These beautiful women are the highlight of the combat scenes, which suffer from an excess of close-up shots and an over-use of slow-motion. The film as a whole is weighed down by its accumulation of clichés (but that is the nature of this 'genre of film'). Alfred Hitchcock considered that a cliché was tolerable as a starting point but not as a conclusion. But Zeb Ejiro, alias 'the Cheikh' slides effortlessly from one cliché to the next, with no pretensions other than to offer a complete diversion from real life.

Date of release: 2004
Filmscript: Kelvin Aladi and Zeb Ejiro
Camera: Steve Oluyede
Cast: Marie Eboka, Festus Aguebor, Osam Isaac, Enebeli Elebuwa, Natty Bruce, Princess 2pee & Augusta Ikhifa
Dialogue in English

1. Tafawa Balewa, Johnson Ironsi, Murtala Mohammed were assassinated. Moshood Abiola was poisoned when he was about to be released from prison. As for Sani Abacha, he wasn't able to survive the cumulative effect of Viagra and two Indian prostitutes (according to the American journalist, Karl Maier, in his book *This House Has Fallen* (Penguin Books: London, 2001)

Filming in Lagos of
The President Must Not Die
(© Jean-Claude Moschetti/REA)

6 Informal Sector or Video 'Industry'?
Pierre Barrot

'Above all, cinema is an industry', said André Malraux. Don Pedro Obaseki, first President of the Filmmakers Cooperative of Nigeria, confirms this in the Nigerian context. 'For many people cinema isn't an art, it is something like an assembly line.' Most distributors have in fact a completely commercial approach and insist on the production team working at an ordered pace. Financial constraints mean that they have to minimize the delay between the expenses paid out for the shoot, the launch of the product on the market and the return on their investment. Tight budgets also mean that everyone has to work as fast as possible. These are not the kind of constraints which help creative talent to blossom. A director such as Lancelot Imasuen, who is among the most talented of the home-video specialists, takes great pride in his prolific output as well as in his capacity to keep to the time-frames imposed by the producers and distributors. Among the film directors profiled in the National Film and Video Censors Board (NFVCB) 2004 directory, Imasuen was the only one to include his complete filmography: 61 full-length feature films on video, by the age of only 31 – quite an achievement.

There is no place in the Nigerian video market for the visionary genius who lets a whim or an idea throw out all production schedules and budgets; it is far from cinema and the playfulness that characterized the early years and its better achievements. The most international of French producers, Daniel Toscan du Plantier, has described of his agonies as a producer when faced with a whimsical and exacting creative talent such as that of the Malian filmmaker Souleymane Cisse. In the middle of shooting the film *Waati* in Côte d'Ivoire, Souleymane called him one day and demanded that he find a lion in France and air-freight it out for the shoot. It took a while for the message to get across that trained animals of this kind were not readily available. But he did manage it – at huge expense.[1]

Nothing like this happens in Nigerian video. With very restricted budgets, each day of filming is counted. A 90-minute feature can be cobbled together in just three days of filming by those most pressed for time. Many Nigerian box-office hits have benefited from ten days filming at most.

1. Souleymane Cissé, whose film *Yeelen* won a prize at the 1987 Cannes Film Festival, has not made another full-length feature film since *Waati* (1995) which was a commercial box-office failure.

Pierre Barrot

Even Tunde Kelani, for all his professionalism, had to be content with 20 days of filming for *The Campus Queen.* But he kept to a non-stop schedule, to keep the team under pressure and to avoid the inevitable delays that come from getting back on track after any interruptions. Even though Kelani considered 20 days not enough time, this period reflects the privileged position of an independent producer, able to set his own demands as a meticulous director who makes only one full-length film a year. Although Kelani is able to be the real creative talent behind his films, most Nigerian film directors are carrying out the demands of a producer, who is often, importantly, also the distributor. More often the directors are given a storyline with all the ingredients considered essential for it to be a hit, actors that they did not chose who will help sell the film, and a draconian production schedule. As in Hollywood, the director doesn't have control over the 'final cut'.[2] It is often difficult when reading the credits of a Nigerian video, to determine who is the 'author' of the film, or who wrote the film script. Between the writer of the storyline who had the original idea, the scriptwriter who has the job of developing that idea, the executive producer, the director and sometimes even a 'technical director', it is often impossible to say who 'owns' the film. The real proprietor is in fact the producer/seller who put up the finance.

It has all the structure of industrial production, but as emphasized by Emmanuel Vincenot, quoted earlier, 'the actual conditions of the directing are still hand-crafted'. Some producers have managed to line up 10 films a year, not one of them has a 'studio' worthy of the name. A hundred films a year come out of the city of Kano, but the number of professional cameras outside the television stations can be counted on one hand. There are probably fewer than in Niamey (Niger), where production is notably absent.

Most of the Nigerian films produced at the beginning of the twenty-first century have been put together on personal computers using Adobe Premiere, which in its early incarnations was closer to an amateur programme than something professional.

This artisanal, or amateurish, production system is matched by low-quality transmission. If the film is only destined to be seen on a small screen, and played through a video-player, then certain technical constraints can be discarded. Broadcast 'norms', as imposed by the television industry of developed countries, do not apply to most Nigerian films. Such standards are crucial for quality television broadcast: the audio and visual signals have to be sent right through to the television viewer by means of transmitters, relay stations and satellites. A low-grade signal will not survive all these obstacles. It will, however, pass from a video-player to a family television without any problem.

Nigerian film producers for the most part are content with poor

2. This is completely different from the French tradition. In Hollywood, control over the final cut belongs to the producer, not the director.

technical standards, because they do not anticipate that their films will be shown either on television or via video-projection onto large screens,

Sound quality, in particular, is sacrificed, even though most of the films are packed with dialogue and people need to understand what the characters are saying. When starting out some directors just use an in-built microphone on the camera to record sound. On most shoots these days there is a sound engineer with a boom but often the positioning of the microphone leaves much to be desired. Above all, the sound engineer does not have enough authority within the film crew to be able to interrupt a shot when the noise of a lorry or a generator drowns out the voice of the actors. Even when the sound recording is good, the dialogue is often ruined by thundering music that does not seem to have been through any balance mix.

The appearance of the commercial channel Africa Magic, a branch of the South African channel M-net, is helping to improve the technical quality of Nigerian films. In buying up hundreds of films, this channel is beleaguered by their poor sound quality. M-Net took the initiative on this and in July 2004 sent two specialists to Lagos to train Nigerian sound-technicians and to try to improve production standards.[3]

Another means of pushing technical standards up is to increase the use of video-projectors. On small screens with a reduced image size and a speaker not much better than that on a television, many imperfections go unnoticed. Despite his cinematic experience, Tunde Kelani admits that he was ashamed during the projection of some of his films at various international film festivals when there were defects in the sound track that he had not noticed beforehand. During the Ouagadougou Pan-African Film Festival 2007, the director Mak Kusare came with a badly mixed tape and had to re-record the sound track for his film *Ninety Degrees* with some speed as it was programmed to go out as part of the festival's video selection.

Even in Nigeria, video-projections were quite rare until recently. The Lagos Film Forum[4] supported since 2001 by the French Embassy, has enabled screenings to take place each year under professional conditions, and above all allows comparison between Nigerian films and films from the rest of the African continent made in 16mm or 35mm formats. In 2004, at the opening of the Film Forum at the Silverbird cinema in Lagos, the head[5] of this new and ultra-modern cinema complex[6] gave a warning to Nigerian producers: there was no question for him of compromising internationally set standards. It was up to Nigerian producers to improve the quality of their films, rather than expect the picture houses to settle for local standards. At least one or two producers took him up on this challenge. Six months later Kingsley Ogoro's film, *Across the Niger*, (the most costly film of all Nigerian video productions up to that time) was premiered in one of the halls of the very same cinema.

3. During its first year of broadcasting this channel only bought films from Southern Nigeria where technical standards are the least poor. In 2005 it started to select Hausa films sub-titled in English. The technical standards of the average Hausa production are even lower, with many films still being made on VHS.
4. Organized by the Independent Television Producers Association of Nigeria (ITPAN).
5. Ben Murray-Bruce, former patron of the national public network.
6. Tickets at this cinema are very expensive (the equivalent of nearly US$ 16 for a full price ticket during the initial launch period and US$ 12 per ticket the following year). It screens mainly American films.

The shooting of What a Shame,
*directed and produced by Franklin
Nwoko, Enugu State, 2006*

(© Robert Minangoy)

There is a long way to go before public screenings are back in the mainstream in Nigeria. The festival organized by the National Film Corporation in December 2003 was marked by some disastrous screenings. It was the same story at the Abuja Film Festival in 2004 (with inaudible sound, poor quality tapes, non-calibrated film, and mobile phones going off in the middle of the screenings). In Nigeria, the absolute predominance of domestic video has led to the disappearance of previous habits and understanding of cinema-going.

Now we are witnessing a revival of cinemas. Since the opening of the Silverbird complex, two others were opened in Lagos in 2005 and 2006 by a Lebanese entrepreneur and the South African company Nu Metro and a number of other projects were announced at the same time in other towns. This development should benefit both celluloid films and the development of video-projections. And this cannot but

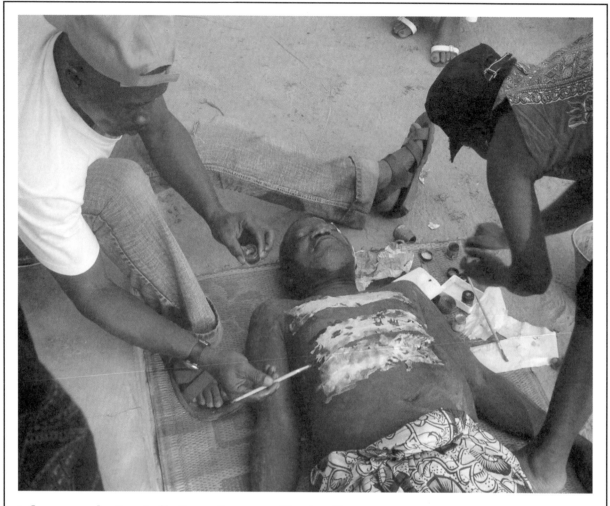

Make-up artists at work on the set of What a Shame, *Enugu State, 2006* (© *Robert Minangoy*)

influence production itself. Currently, many Nigerian films are not made for the cinema. Many just fizzle out at the end simply because the producer-distributors decided in the editing process to stretch the film out by cutting it in two. They can sell two V-CDs instead of one, thereby increasing profits. This way of doing things is adapted to video, not to cinema outlets.

In countries where production is aimed mostly at cinema screenings, public access to the films is limited by the number of screens available. What we see is that most box-office sales are limited to a number of 'blockbusters'. In 2003, in France, an American film exceeded the symbolic threshold of a thousand copies of the film distributed. This event led to a controversy which set independent producers against certain distributors, who were accused of duplicating copies in order to 'fill up' the largest possible number of screens, to the

Pierre Barrot

7. According to the manifesto 'Libérons les écrans' denouncing the increase in the number of prints of big budget films, on 2 January 2004, just three American films and one French film were filling 3,022 of the 5,280 screens available in France.
8. In relation to his film *Aba Women Riot*, Eddie Ugbomah recalls: 'The producers said that I should re-shoot it and add some blood and some violence. I refused. So that after spending 1.2 million Naira, the film has never been released.' (quote from Okoh Aihie's, *African Movie Directors in Their Own Words*, National Film Institute, Jos, Nigeria, 2004.
9. Even though less in evidence than in cinematographic productions, French involvement is still common in a large proportion of the television series produced in francophone Africa during the first few years of this century (*A nous la vie, Au Royaume d'Abou, Les Bobodioufs, Kadi Jolie, Monia et Rama, Les aventures de Seko, Taxi Brousse, Fables à l'usage des Blancs en Afrique*). Such dependency doesn't exist at all in Nigeria. When the British director Nick Moran came to Lagos in 2003 to make a documentary about Nollywood and the Nigerian home-video industry, Jeta Amata who was supposed to just assist him, took charge and directed the home-video *Game of Life*. After this experience, Moran said to his Nigerian colleagues 'They could work anywhere in the world. I think if you took Jeta [Amata] and Stella [Damasus-Aboderin] and put them on a plane to London or Los Angeles, they would get work.' One year later, Jeta Amata engaged Nick Moran as an actor in *Amazing Grace*, which was the first 35mm film to have been made in Nigeria since 1992. The film, edited in Los Angeles, was screened for the first time at the Cannes Film Festival in 2006 (see Epilogue, p. 132).

detriment of low budget films.[7] This situation is seen as damaging any possible diversity in cinematographic production.

In Nigeria there is no danger of this happening yet. With distribution concentrated exclusively on video, there is no physical limit to the number of video copies that can be made: a lesser known title can always find a corner of a shelf in the video-stores, even though it would probably never be given a screen in a cinema. Even if cinematic showings make a come-back in Nigeria, there is very little chance that it will lead to a reduction in the number of films made, or lead to a concentration of budgets on fewer but higher quality productions, as some people would like. In the 2004 *Film and Video Directory*, Rosalyn Odeh, former director of the NFVCB, expressed this wish:

> If we make 200 films a year, this would be better for us than wasting all our time and resources on 2,000 'rubbish films'. This sort of proliferation will only be to the detriment of our film industry.

The proliferation of 'rubbish' is the price of diversity. It is also the price paid for the amount of freedom which Nigerian video producers enjoy. It is true that the directors operate under a great number of constraints and many are victims of the kind of formula inflicted on them by the promoters: celebrities and violence.[8] But they are still less restricted and less driven to self-censorship than television producers.

Being prolific has another advantage. It gives an opportunity to a large number of people who are self-taught and would never have the opportunity to express themselves in a more professional and better organised system. In francophone Africa, the small output and the fact that cinema is used as the point of reference limits the chances of nurturing young talent. Only through access to a recognized training can the beginnings of a talent begin to emerge. Because of this, video production in francophone Africa still makes use of a large number of French technicians, writers and directors.[9]

The fact that Nigeria (in contrast to countries like Brazil or India) doesn't have any large studios, just a multitude of small 'artisans-bricoleurs' has guaranteed not only its diversity but also its authenticity.

Nigerian video is the equivalent of the 'informal sector' in African manufacturing. There is an impressive resistance to being structured, constrained and having to adhere to norms. When the video distributors imposed a boycott on the highest paid stars, they put the brakes on budgetary inflation, thus putting off the threat of investors who might come in, dominate the market and eliminate the 'small', low-budget producers. By remaining hand-crafted, dispersed and barely professional, video production keeps its more spontaneous character and remains closer to the public than televised productions or African cinema. Its eccentric, if not anarchic character also prevents the video phenomenon from being controlled by outside forces. It is this aspect that makes it different from another kind of production which is equally popular in Africa: South American soap-operas. These programmes emanate from some of the giants of television[10] and represent for some critics, a means of conditioning the population. According to sociologist Inez Da Silva,[11] these soap-operas were used in Brazil as 'the opiate of the people' during the period of military rule. She says that they are still a means of social control today in the service of the established order, publicity people and presenters. Black actors are hardly ever seen in roles outside of the domestic; other ills of Brazilian society are also not discussed in the soap-operas. They are literally a 'diversion' (in the sense of turning people's attention away from real life).

Even though Nigerian video production also calls itself 'an entertainment industry', it does not have the same anaesthetic quality as 'telenovelas', and it does not turn its back on the ills of Nigerian society. On the contrary it delights in them, exploits them, denounces or exorcises them; whatever the problem, it is dealt with in the greatest detail.

Inez Da Silva observes, again in relation to the soap-operas: 'In Brazil there are more televisions than refrigerators.' What she is implying is that conditioning people's minds is more important than developing them. It is most likely that in Nigeria, in an even more shocking way, the number of video-players outnumbers not just refrigerators, but also taps with drinking water, or even mosquito nets. What is certain, is that there are more tapes and V-CDs than there are school text books.

However, perhaps in a few years there will be a transformation in Nigerian society. And who knows whether the creators of video-films will not have contributed as much, if not more, than the teachers?

Many intellectuals make the mistake of considering the most popular leisure activities to be futile and detrimental. Such an error of judgement was summed up perfectly by Umberto Eco when he said: 'Television stupefies cultivated people and cultivates people who have a stupifying life.' The same thing could be said of Nigerian videos.

10. TV Globo in Brazil, and TV Azteca in Mexico.
11. Statement during a television workshop at the Lagunimages Festival, Cotonou, 2002.

Film Profile No. 6
The Mourning After
Directed by Jimi Odumosu

Date of release: 2004
Production: Lagos Television and Uhuru Productions
Filmscript: Jimi Odumosu
Cast: Bimbo Akintola, Zainab Buki-Ajayi, Perpetua Uku, Victor Eze, Ahmed Yerima & Charles Ukpong
Dialogue in English

Bisi, a cardiologist from Lagos, lives the stressful but full life of a modern woman, successful in her career and loved by her husband and two daughters, the youngest of whom, Tobi, is at high school. Her only frustration is that she has never been able to have a son in nearly 20 years of marriage. The very moment she discovers that she is pregnant and that her wish has finally been granted, her husband is so overcome that he is struck down with a heart attack. Overwhelmed with grief, Bisi agrees to go to her deceased husband's village in the South East of Nigeria for the condolence ceremonies. She doesn't suspect the horrible web of circumstances in which the traditional belief system will ensnare her.

Without being a 're-make', this film takes up the same theme (the merciless treatment inflicted on widows in many parts of Africa) and uses the same actors who were in Tade Ogidan's *Saving Alero* (released in 2000).

Despite the quality of the latter, *The Mourning After* achieves an even higher standard, thanks to the very different production conditions. Jimi Odumosu shot the film while he was in post as Head of Television for Lagos State. *The Mourning After* was therefore produced outside of the usual context of the home-video industry and escaped the stringencies of rapid release which restricts any possibility of script development and affects the amount of post-production work on most Nigerian films. While Tade Ogidan had to condense the filming of *Saving Alero* into three weeks, Jimi Odumosu had to extend that of *The Mourning After* to nearly six months because of his lack of availability. He worked on script development by himself with slow adjustments over a long period. Thus the story and his capturing of it on screen had a long maturation, which is very rare in Nigerian video-production. 'Most directors', explains Jimi Odumosu, 'are detached from their storyline. In order to make a good film, you need to be involved in it, to live it, inside, before filming it.[1]

Perhaps because of its long maturation *The Mourning After* has, as well as its emotional impact, a poetic dimension rarely present in Nigerian films. There is, for example, the surprising scene of 'dialogue'

1. Interview carried out on 19 October 2004.

between Bimbo Akintola, who is being kept in solitary confinement in a small hut, and her only visitor – a cockroach, memorable for its lustrous body.

One of the most powerful scenes of the film, Bisi's trial in the middle of the night by a village tribunal, was filmed in a studio, which is also exceptional in Nigerian production. The result is that a particularly tense atmosphere is created. One of the actors, Charles Ukpong, claims to having been put in the mood by the set design and confined atmosphere of the studio, which went perfectly with the sense of being suddenly and totally cut off from the world. This is Bisi's experience, most effectively conveyed to and shared by the audience.

The village and its traditions reveal a different world and another time-frame. The great strength of Jimi Odumosu's film is his ability to make the heroine's feeling of confinement and the loss of bearings palpable. She is confronted with another universe, unalterable and implacable, that she, coming from Lagos and its whirlwind of urban life, never suspected was there.

Another strength of the film is the resistance led by Bisi's daughter Tobi, which Jimi Odumosu puts forward as 'an example of the appeal to civil society, for non-violence, for negotiation'. Here again, the content and power of the message is exceptionally well presented.

7 Jumping on the Bandwagon
Tunde Oladunjoye

<<<<<<<<<<<<<<<<<<<<<<<<<<<<<<<<<<<<<<<<<<<<<<<<<<<

It is easier to understand how performance and theatre as industries have carved their own path in Nigeria if one traces its origins back to the Yoruba travelling theatre troupes such as 'Agbegijo and the Anarejo' who brought theatre to the people, along with Duro Ladipo, Ishola Ogunmola, Lere Paimo, Oyin Adejobi and many other theatrical troupes from the beginning of the 1950s. Following this was a period which included the films of Hubert Ogunde, Moses Olaiya and Jab Adu at the start of the 1970s – a tradition culminating in the videos made by Idumota and Iweka,

The video-film business whose early exponents were considered to be lazy, illiterate and of low morals, can today be proud to have in its ranks not only educated, well-travelled professionals but also very wealthy producers, distributors and directors, and the most sought after actors and actresses. It is estimated that annual turnover for the industry is now 20 billion Naira and that it employs 200,000 people.

As cultural, political and economic aspects of a country's development are interlinked, it is impossible to separate the development of the Nigerian cinematographic industry from the economic, political and social realities on the ground. During the oil boom of the 1970s (a favourable period economically, despite the presence of a military regime and the fact that the country had only just come out of a three-year civil war), the film industry prospered. There were large cinemas, run for the most part by Lebanese, in the main towns and cities of Lagos, Ibadan, Kano and Jos.

The economy collapsed with the end of the oil boom. Policies of 'Nigerianization' and nationalization (which, in retrospect, were just an example of the military's ill-conceived populist reforms), led a vast number of foreigners to leave the country and invest their money elsewhere. The price of consumer goods and of imported equipment increased considerably. Nigerian filmmakers were unable to hold out against the serious economic conditions and had to find other solutions.

 Home-video arrived just at the right time, because people had begun to be more housebound as the security situation worsened and

standards of living fell. Many families could no longer afford the luxury of going to the cinema. Nigerians turned to the sentimentality of television serials such as *Behind the Cloud, Mirror in the Sun, Checkmate, Mega Fortune* among others that were broadcast primarily on NTA (the Nigerian Television Authority, the federal public television channel).

As a consequence, when Kenneth Nnebue gathered together some of the stars from these television series to make *Living in Bondage*, the film became an instant success. Subsequently Amaka Igwe made *Rattlesnake*, and in a very short time, everybody wanted to make home-videos. This aspiration was given impetus by the fact that the market for electronic equipment and VHS video players was already well-established in Idumota, on Lagos Island. The video-film market then extended to Iweka Rd, Onitsha, Aba and to Eastern Nigeria, until 2003, when some producers left Idumota, to set up a new, modern marketplace in Surulere, under the auspices of the Filmmakers Cooperative of Nigeria.

The market in video developed despite the initially unenthusiastic attitude of the authorities. Today, those involved are proud to present the video sector as the first (and perhaps only) enterprise that can restore Nigeria's image in the outside world. According to Don Pedro Obaseki, a well-known Nigerian filmmaker, who was President of the Filmmakers Cooperative of Nigeria:

> These days, films are the best way of promoting Nigeria. Two years ago I was in Liberia interviewing some of the rebel leaders. They took me to a remote place in the north of the country. In the middle of the bush they got out a video-player, a television, and, incredibly, started showing Nigerian films. Previously, if you went abroad people would ask if you had brought food or spices from home. Today they ask if you have brought any Nigerian films.

At the border posts between Nigeria and Niger, traffickers offer Nigerian video-films to the customs officers as bribes, and this is how the films were introduced to Niger.

It is easier to extract water from a stone that to get reliable statistics on the home-video industry in Nigeria. Even the sector's own regulatory and monitoring bodies only work from estimates and guesswork about its size. If you ask a producer for the production cost of a film, or for the amount of fees that each actor earned, invariably the answer will be: 'This is top secret information! We don't give away the secrets of our trade.' Such attitudes are harmful to the growth of the sector as it is difficult to make a reliable plan without good figures.

It is estimated that the number of video-clubs distributed across the 36 states of Nigeria is 23,000, of which less than 3,000 are officially registered with the Board of Censors. Video-clubs, which are accused by the producers of inhibiting the development of the industry, rent out a film on VHS or V-CD for 50 Naira. In most cases the cost of producing a 90-minute home-video, shot over seven days, is one million Naira ($US 8,000).

The themes of the films do not vary much. One critic claimed with some exaggeration that if you have seen one Nigerian video then you have seen them all. This is what Adams Omoosun, Head of Operations at Infinity Merchant Films calls 'the bandwagon effect'. The Director-General of Videofield Company, Emmanuel Isikaku, is of the same opinion:

> In this sector, there is a worrying tendency. When a storyline goes down well, everyone jumps on the same idea. Competition is fierce. There was a time when love stories were the thing, with silly titles and plots.

Abosede Francis, one of the managers of the Lagos regional office of the NFVCB, sums up the situation:

> Most of the plots are the same and one ends up getting bored. For example, if one person releases a film called *Genesis of Blood* and it is a hit, a large number of producers throw themselves behind the theme and bring out films with such titles as *Origin of Blood, Beginning of Blood, Start of Blood, Birth of Blood*, etc, which are purely and simply repeats of the plot of the original *Genesis of Blood*.

There is little creativity in the film themes: fears, legends, superstitions, witchcraft, the occult, violence, etc. Certain themes and subject matter lead to disputes between the monitoring bodies (the National Board of Censors) and the video-makers. The Censorship Board justifies its interventions against 'the persistence of certain negative cultural practices' (as stated by Rosalyn Odeh, Director of NFVCB until 2005, in an interview given to *Tell* magazine).

Even in countries where traditional religions are considered among the official religions (no doubt she is referring here to Benin, where the calendar of public holidays includes a 'day for traditional religions'), Rosalyn Odeh insists that the films of that country should not address the subject. However, Don Pedro Obaseki thinks that the NFVCB should not get involved with regulating films. According to him, censorship is a product of dictatorship, and art should not be censored. In his opinion the Censors Board should be re-named the 'Film Classification Board'.

The first Vice-President of the Onitsha section of the Association of Film and Video Marketers (the Association of Film and Video Distributors), Rob Emeka Eze was also opposed to the ideas of Rosalyn Odeh:

> The Board keeps talking about suppressing this and that! It is killing the producers' creativity, when they are told to cut certain scenes

Yoruba language films represent one-third of all production
(© Jean-Claude Moschetti/REA)

from their films. If you are making a historic film about war or insurrection, you can't clean it up just to please the censors.

In Kano (the centre of the industry in Northern Nigeria), censorship is even stricter than in the rest of the country. However, it is interesting to note that local film production does well compared to that in other regions. This is due to the influence of Indian films and to the enthusiastic and entrepreneurial activity of its supporters, despite the fact that their level of training is poor.

Even though there is a regional office of the NFVCB in Kano, the State authorities, on 13 December 2000, also established its own Board of Censors with 16 members. This was a consequence of the establishment of Sharia law as the legal framework.[1] As well as dealing with films, this local office regulates people running cybercafés, who are only authorized to allow customers access to 'approved websites'.

After the establishment of Sharia law, nearly all the cinemas in Kano were closed down. They could not re-open until several months later, and then under heavy restrictions imposed by the promoters: strict separation of men from women, much higher sanitation

1. Sharia law existed previously alongside the federal judicial system, but it was only applied in cases of family litigation or disputes over land.

standards (hygiene, lighting and a 'safe' distance between the male and female toilets). Moreover, the cinemas had, from then on, to keep to a quota of showing 40 per cent of local Hausa films.e

Predictably, instead of complicating their lives by adhering to the standards of separation required by the Board of Censors, the promoters simply prohibited women from coming to the cinemas. The result in Kano today is that the Marhaba cinema – the biggest and most popular with seating for about 1,500 people – is three-quarters empty, while hundreds of young girls hang around in the small cafés nearby.

Ali Bature, one of the managers of the Office for Arts and Culture for Kano State, admits that it is currently very difficult to comply with the new directives. However, their disastrous consequences are already evident. The number of films being produced in Northern Nigeria has dropped considerably, whereas before 2001 when the introduction of Sharia law began to make an impact, the region used to be the foremost producer of films in local languages.[2]

For professional filmmakers trying to work in the North, Sharia law is one more problem to add to the other nationwide scourge – piracy. Producers, the NFVCB and other partners are all in agreement: the agents charged with fighting piracy are, without doubt, not sufficiently intent on stopping it, or have been left behind, as the producers are, by the sophisticated methods and intense secrecy at the heart of the network. Piracy makes maximum use of the new technologies available, in communications (such as the internet), as well as in the counterfeiting and duplication of copies. In answer to the question 'How can we fight the activities of the pirates?', Socrate Safo, a Ghanaian video-filmmaker replies: 'Nobody can fight the pirates. The only thing we can do is try to undermine them.'

When the Motion Picture Practitioners Association (MOPPAN) decided to fight both the selling of pirated copies and the illegal exploitation of video-clubs, they ran up against the following charge: if you end piracy you put 20,000 people in Kano out of work.[3]

Piracy is an international phenomenon, and because of the lack of cooperation between the networks of Nigerian video-makers and their partners abroad, annual losses are considerable. For example, it is estimated that between 500 and 1,000 new Nigerian films go into Kenya every year, which is 60 per cent of the total number of tapes and V-CDs sold in the country, at a turnover of between US$ 3 million and US$ 6 million. Unfortunately, there isn't an agreement between the Nigerian distributors and their Kenyan counterparts. Most of these Nigerian videos are in fact pirate copies and are smuggled into Kenya. The customs authorities do not have reliable figures available and the agencies fighting piracy lose their cases in court because they do not even get the support of the producers or creators of the pirated material.

2. Among the 750 films monitored by the Censors Board in the year 2000, 187 of these were in Hausa, compared to only 160 in the Yoruba language. The number of films in Hausa fell to 76 in 2003, whereas in the same year 193 films in Yoruba were monitored.
3. Anecdote reported by Hamisu Iyan-Tama, President of the Arewa Film Producers Association, which represents the film producers of Northern Nigeria.

In Ghana, piracy is as bad as in Nigeria. Even the legally registered distributors are involved. The Nigerian owner of the company Atlantis Film Productions was arrested at the end of 2003 for having pirated 12 films belonging to the Ghanaian production company, Silverline.

Samuel Kwesi Bruce is Director-General of Palma Video Production and also an executive member of the Film and Video Distributors Association in Ghana. He explains that the Association tries to fight piracy with the help of the police:

> We make enquiries and we identify anything that seems suspect to the Association. We also try to change the colours and logos on the video-cassettes to try to thwart the pirates ['cut the grass under their feet'].

Adams Omoosun, from Infinity Merchants Limited, uses the same tactic in Nigeria: 'I have already tried this approach and it worked well in Ijora and Alaba [markets in Lagos], which are the big centres for piracy', but he added:

> Don't forget that the pirates are able to make copies that are better than the originals. Another effective strategy for us is to flood the markets with tapes or CDs so we beat the pirates to it.

Socrate Safo, the Ghanaian producer cited above, agrees:

> It is a matter of watching what success the films have and which are in demand at any one time. If you don't manage to satisfy the demand, then the way is open for pirates. All you have to do is release a sufficiently large number of copies at the time a film is first screened.

Opinions are divided and contradictory about the role of state intervention. They fall into three categories. The first group thinks that the home-video industry is part of the private sector and that the state should have nothing to do with it. The second group favours state intervention limited to giving support to the infrastructures needed. The third group thinks that the state should step in to control the sector, given its importance for the country's image and the influence of its output in the political and socio-cultural domain. The President of Nigeria, Olusegun Obasanjo, indicated in his budget speech of 2003 that home-video was one of the areas that he planned to develop, because of its income-generating and employment capacity.

In the first instance, nothing concrete was done to honour this presidential promise. On the contrary, the two federal agencies concerned with the film industry, the Nigerian National Film Corporation (NFC) and the NFVCB, became involved in pointless competition with each other. The NFC organized the Second National Cinema Festival at the end of 2003, rather misleadingly, since it was about 11 years after the first festival.

The award ceremony organized the same year by the NFVCB made a bit more of an impression due to the presence of political big-wigs and by the donation of the one million Naira prize, put up by the Governor of Rivers State, Peter Odili, and won by the film *Peacemaker*. But many critics, such as the journalist Uche Nnadozie asked why a Board of Censors had anything to do with the organization of the film industry's award-ceremonies.

In order to promote the development of the sector, professionals in the industry created a number of organizations: the Filmmakers Cooperative of Nigeria, the Motion Pictures Practitioners Association (MOPPAN), the Independent Television Producers Association of Nigeria (ITPAN), the Actors Guild, and the Dancers Guild, among others.[4] These organizations contribute to the improvement and regulation of the film industry but their work remains limited to video production. Not a single Nigerian producer released a full-length 35mm feature film between 1994 and 2006. (Ladi Ladebo shot *Heritage*, in 'Super 16' in 2001 but he could only edit this film on digital video. The Nigerian Film Corporation made *Zanani* in 2002, but were never able to release a satisfactory version of this film). Main obstacles are the lack of financial support and the poor condition of the infrastructures (the laboratory of the National Film Corporation in Jos doesn't inspire confidence in filmmakers such as Ladi Ladebo, who lost metres of the film stock there). And as the big international film festivals give greater importance to celluloid films, 'small' countries such as Burkina Faso fare better than the 'giant of Africa' in the showcase of international filmmakers.

Newton Aduaka, a Nigerian filmmaker based in Paris, addresses this issue:

> I think we are largely responsible for this situation as opportunities for Nigerian filmmakers to make films in celluloid do exist. There is the European Commission fund, which gives out considerable sums of money each year to Burkina Faso, Senegal, Mauritania, Chad and Niger. We don't even ask; the funds that do exist are not even applied for. Ladi Ladebo was the only person to submit a project in the last few years. That's our problem. If we really want to make films, we need to approach these funds in the way the francophone countries do.[5]

But in Nigeria some people consider any financial or other support given by international organizations as a way of facilitating foreign control. This was the subject of fierce debate in the monthly sessions of the Lagos branch of the Association of Nigerian Authors (ANA) in June 2004. The gathering was divided into two camps, each as vocal as the other. One group maintained that funding is only given to writers who ridicule their own country and society; the others were of

4. There is even a Stuntsman's Guild.
5. Newton Aduaka was given Euros 100, 000 by the European Union, and Euros 205,000 by two French funding bodies, for his full-length film *Waiting for an Angel*.

the opinion that artists shouldn't be afraid of telling things the way they are. Writers, producers and other artists, who agree to sacrifice their independence and accept private, public or international sponsorship, are responsible for their own choices. As Adams Omoosun concludes:

> Producers and directors need to behave like professionals and to know how to resist unjustified pressures. Some well-known producers, such as Tade Ogidan, are wedded to working professionally. Tade Ogidan would not accept having someone else's view imposed on him.

Film Profile No. 7
Thunderbolt (Magun)
Directed by Tunde Kelani

Date of release: 2000
Production: Mainframe
Fimscript: Femi Kayode (based
on the novel *Magun* by
Adebayo Faleti)
Editing: Wale Kelani
Cast: Uche Obi-Osotule, Lanre
Balogun, Zainab Buki-Ajayi,
Wale Macaulay, Larinde
Akinleye & Ngozi Nwosu
Dialogue in English

Ngozi is a young Igbo woman who is married to a Yoruba. While she works towards her civil service qualifications in a school situated about 100 km from her husband's home, her husband begins to be tormented by jealousy. Mortified by his suspicions, Ngozi becomes increasingly unhappy. One day she is approached by a strange, ghost-like old man. The apparition reveals that she has been cast a terrible fate: the *magun*. Every woman struck by this curse is incapable of having sex with a man without that man being struck down dead. Even if she remains faithful, she herself will die nine weeks later.

Tortured and agonized, Ngozi lets her landlady drive her to see some fetishists who will try to undo the spell. Despite her disgust with the process, the treatment seems to be effective. But the healers announce that in order for the *magun* to be totally eradicated, she will have to undergo one last 'test': Ngozi must have sex with one man of her choosing. Given the risks involved in this, the act has to be performed under the watchful eyes of the healers...

This story, which can seem a bit on the indelicate side, was adapted with great subtlety by Femi Kayode (one of the top Nigerian filmmakers) and resulted in one of the most beautiful of Tunde Kelani's films. Far from being the bawdy farce which you might expect (the Yoruba word *magun* literally meaning 'a person forbidden from mounting'), the film deals delicately with the pitfalls of married life, and also the power of popular beliefs. Uche Obi-Osotule is so caught up in her character that she frequently bursts into real tears, with no hint of artificiality, and by doing so manages to convey an irresistible level of emotion.

The end of the film (an astonishing duel between traditional healers and western medicine) is resolved with victory to the fetishists. This conclusion seems to be a concession by Tunde Kelani to his Yoruba public, the majority of whom are raised within traditional belief systems. Rather than demystify what he regards as superstition, Tunde Kelani seems to bring his own warning about the myth of *magun*. He explains it thus: that his idea is not to glorify traditional medicine but to suggest to the gurus of western medicine that they would benefit from being more open to the knowledge of traditional healers. According to Kelani, this approach, combining curiosity and modesty, exists in South Africa but is cruelly lacking in Nigeria).

Like all Tunde Kelani's films, *Thunderbolt* is a truly cinematographic production, even though it was shot on video. Its creator has been Director of Photography on a number of celluloid films and brings with him a real concern for the quality of the shots, for the lighting and the sets, which is recognizable as his trademark in all his film projects.

The music by Tunde Oyelana, who Tunde Kelani brought especially from London to record, gives the film its strong sense of melancholy, as spell-binding as the *magun* itself.

8 Nigerian Video as the 'Child of Television'
Don Pedro Obaseki[1]

It is important to understand that the way the home-video phenomenon in Nigeria has developed, is quite different from that of cinema in Nigeria. In most of the fora that I have attended, people think that the home-video industry is an offshoot of cinema, which is quite incorrect. The Yoruba travelling theatre, the Agbegijo and Aberejo, produced a popular travelling art form. This tradition began at the time of the fall of the old Oyo Empire and it metamorphosed into the travelling theatre of Hubert Ogunde, Duro Ladipo, Kola Ogunmola and others. When these theatre practitioners started making films, we saw the creation of films by Baba Sala (whose real name is Moses Olaiya), Ladi Ladebo, Mose Bolatan and one by Ogunde called *Bread and Bullet.*

However, when it came to the mid-1970s, after the indigenization decree (initiated during the Obasanjo military regime) there was a dearth of cinematic film screenings. Most of the cinemas were owned by Lebanese; after the indigenization decree, there was the push by Nigerians to own cinemas. This reduced the level of ownership by the Lebanese, who then stopped importing films, predominantly cowboy/ westerns, Indian, and Chinese films.

With the introduction of Structural Adjustment Programmes (SAPs) by the Ibrahim Babangida military regime in 1986, Nigerians were no longer able to import films. Those who were making films at that time were Chief Eddy Ugbomah, Ola Balogun, Ladi Ladebo, Jab Adu (creator of *Bisi, Daughter of the River*) and even, in the early 1980s, Wole Soyinka (for example his *Blues for the Prodigal*).

It had become difficult for such films to be screened, or even shot in the first place, because of foreign exchange constraints. But the home-video industry as we know it today developed out of this crisis. But it metamorphosed from television: it is the child of television, not of film.

Structural Adjustment Programmes killed off the culture of cinema. The filmmakers who could make the crossover were rare. Directors such as Tunde Kelani who used to shoot on celluloid now had to shoot on video. He made a success of this transition with films like *Thunderbolt* and *Agogo Eewo.*

In the late 1980s, we used to assign our students to work with Zeb

1. These observations by Don Pedro Obaseki were taken down during an interview with Tunde Oladunjoye.

Editing a Hausa language film in Kano

(© Frédéric Noy)

Ejiro, who at that time had the longest running soap in the country, *Ripples*. Another mentor was Amaka Igwe who also had a long run with *Checkmate*. These two soaps were the successors to Matt Dadzie's *Behind the Cloud* (made in Northern Nigeria) and Lola Fani-Kayode's *Mirror in the Sun*.

Ralph Nwadike, one of the producers of the soaps *Ripples*, *Checkmate* and *Mega Fortune*, unfortunately had a problem with the Nigerian Television Authority (NTA), who wanted the sponsors to pay them directly, and to claim back ownership of the programmes. At the same time, the companies that sponsored these programmes – Lever Brothers and Paterson Zochonis – had problems with Lintas Advertising and Insight Communications, the advertising agencies, as they were not passing on to Amaka Igwe and Zeb Ejiro the money that was due to them. There was a breakdown of relations between the parties, and as a result Nigerians were left with numerous stars who had been created by television but whose programmes were no longer running, for example, Nobert Young, Pete Edochie and Fred Amata.

A certain Kenneth Nnebue, who had been making short films with the Yoruba, along with Sam Azubuike and a few of others (who had been shooting films with VHS cameras), decided to work with some of these established television stars who were already familiar to the viewers. They decided to produce a soap that would be distributed on video-cassettes, as the television channels were no longer broadcasting Nigerian soap operas. To fill the gap, NTA had started importing Mexican soaps such as *The Rich Also Cry*, *No One But You* and *Wild Rose*.

Kenneth Nnebue took the TV superstars Richard Mofe Damijo, Segun Arinze, Fred Amata, Bob Manuel-Udokwu, Kenneth Okonkwo, Liz Benson, and many more, and shot *Living in Bondage*. A particular section of Nnamdi Azikiwe Street and Ereko Lane in Idumota (a busy and thriving Lagos business district) were the places that specialized in selling video-cassettes and video-players. It is easy to understand how the people who sold video-players then became the distributors, as they had the necessary equipment for duplication of copies. Not long after that, Amaka Igwe shot *Rattlesnake*. Then more and more people got involved with making films. This was how the thing got started – using the stars that television had made so popular.

The industry evolved without any government or even private sector intervention such as the banking sector. It just appeared in a very informal, almost accidental way that wasn't at all structured. This is why we still have lots of problems.

During this whole period, the Yoruba 'travelling cinema' continued, even if it was restricted to one ethnic region. Nobody can claim credit for that. After the disappearance of the likes of Baba Sala and the death of Ojo Ladipo, members of their troupes became superstars in their own right. That was how stars such as Papi Luwe, Oga Bello and Madam Awero came about. Only Sam Loco Efe was able to complete the circle: from stage to film, film to video, video to television, before returning to the stage. He became a superstar in Nigeria in 1977 playing the lead role as the young Akaraogun in Wale Ogunyemi's *Langbodo*.

There are a few of us who are trying to revive cinema and the cinema-going culture in Nigeria. The situation in Northern Nigeria demonstrates this. The social structure up there is able to support cinema. It is a lot safer to venture out at night. The only danger might come from religious conflicts, but these do not happen very often. Even when they do occur, people still go to the cinema. In the South, cinemas still exist but not to the extent that they used to. The Yoruba travelling theatre continues to screen films at the National Arts Theatre in Lagos. As to the home-video sector – it cannot really be accused of abandoning cinema, it just never really used it. You can only abandon something if you once owned it.

People were lured away from cinema by insecurity. At the end of the 1980s and beginning of the 1990s, during the time of the Structural Adjustment Programme and the Babangida regime, the level of insecurity had reached its zenith, so that people no longer went out. The home-video phenomenon was a practical response because almost everybody had a video-player, and they could watch films at home. Nevertheless, going to the cinema has a magic of its own that video machine cannot replace; it is like a communion. I am confident that cinemas are coming back. In 2004 we had the opening of the Silverbird cinema complex in Lagos. The South Africans have also begun to develop their own projects. Things are changing.

In the last nine years, I have been in the thick of this business. I have had my fingers burnt just like some other distributors. I don't think, however, that the distributors have done anything wrong. They can be reproached for all kinds of things, but it is important to remember the saying that 'he who pays the piper that calls the tune'. Many of our colleagues, both producers and directors, have some responsibility for the way the distributors have taken control. In the past a lot of them had cheated money out of our friends in Idumota. At that time, many of them were not producing films but were just buying the rights. Some producers went as far as selling the rights of the same film to three different people. It's a truly Nigerian phenomenon.

In reaction against such blatant dishonesty, many distributors decided to control both the production and the content of the films. As a result, they went from being tape-sellers to executive producers, in effect.

Today we have a choice, whereas before there was none. It is as if it had all been planned. Either you had to release your film through the prevailing system or be condemned to doing nothing. That is why we came up with the Surulere Film Market, which is owned and operated by the Filmmakers Cooperative of Nigeria. We wanted a place where we had some possibility of controlling events. Most of us have our businesses in Surulere, a neighbourhood a bit like Nigeria's 'Hollywood'. Everybody who owns a film company in Nigeria is part of the Filmmakers Cooperative.

Filmmakers, not distributors, run the film market here. In the Filmmakers Cooperative of Nigeria, we have Tade Ogidan, Mahmood Ali-Balogun, Tunde Kelani, Teco Benson, Charles Novia, Zack Orji, Olu Jacobs, Ramsey Nouah, Fred Amata, Ralph Nwadike, Kingsley Ogoro, etc. Nearly all of them are also actors.

We've been doing this business for ten years without being able to take visitors to the place where we sell our tapes. When people visit from abroad, we can't take them to Idumota.

Furthermore, we decided to build the film market in Surulere with some class. What we want above all is some glamour. We want to avoid going into places like Idumota where you have to walk about in the mud and among the dregs of society. We had to take the future of our profession into our own hands. In economic terms, to be able to

Don Pedro Obaseki

control production, you have to own the means of production. And to get there you also have to control the distribution networks. This is why we have built 30 shops to date and intend to build 30 more, plus a warehouse.

Our aim is also to control the market. If you supply too many films there will be a fall in sales. We have decided that none of us will release more than five films per year. We are all interested in quality control, so we have set up a Quality Control Committee, headed by Mahmood Ali Balogun, and a Committee for the Control of Film Releases, headed by Teco Benson.

The Governor of Lagos State has also given us by 20 hectares of land in Epe, where we have decided to build a 'Film Village'.

Film is a cultural weapon; it is also an imperialist instrument. As an Edo man (from the Benin City region), it goes without saying that I will not put money into a film that is a panegyric to Ijebu culture. It would be easier to convince me to do a film about Benin than one on the Ijebus. In the same way, you won't find Yoruba films today talking about Igbo people.[2] If an American is doing a film about Nigeria, he will do it in such a way that will emphasize American hegemony. Film is a malleable cultural tool. It can be used for propaganda. It is an excellent tool for colonizing peoples. The *oyinbo* (whites) used it in this way.

I wrote and directed *Igodo*, perhaps one of the most important films on Igbo culture. But the film was written from Benin; for two years I looked for funding for the film but nobody from Benin was ready to put money into it. In the end, an Igbo agreed to finance it, so all the locals, the Adesuwas, the Osagies changed names to Ogbonna, Okeke and Uchenna.[3] Moreover, *Igodo*, the original title from the Benin language was now pronounced in the Igbo way, and with this slight variation in pronunciation meant 'chains', which had nothing to do with the story at all.

But despite all this I wrote *Igodo* and it was a success. Subsequently there were hundreds of imitations of the film, mere shadows of the original. Each successful film becomes a locomotive and everyone tries to attach their own wagon to the back of it. Everybody hops on the bandwagon: for a lot of people, cinema is no longer an art form, but just an assembly line.

2. Tunde Kelani's film *Thunderbolt* is an exception to this, and he complained that the distributors (the majority of whom are Igbo) were cool towards this film which had one of its ethnic group as its heroine. According to Tunde Kelani, the distributors were afraid that a Yoruba producer was encroaching on the Igbo clientele, which they considered as their own 'closed market'.
3. Common Igbo first names.

Film Profile No. 8
Jealous Lovers
Directed by Adim Williams

Chioma (played by Geneviève Nnaji) loves her fiancé Nonso but he is showing signs of increasing jealousy and violent behaviour. Their frequent rows provoke a brutal reaction from Chioma's brothers, who persuade her to break up with Nonos, even though she still loves him. Chioma is then courted by a rich industrialist, then by a drug addict rapper (played by Jim Iyke, even more of a hooligan than usual). One day she discovers that Nonso, her old fiancé, was deceived into jealousy by one of her cousins, who had been slandering her behind her back.

Jealous Lovers is a perfect example of Nigerian home-video: filmed for the most part with a hand-held camera, with a minimum of editing, with dialogues that are often too long. But the actors bring an energy and a joy to their roles which is refreshing. There is a particularly impressive sequence in which Geneviève Nnaji resists the advances of an obese millionaire who is sprawled in the back of his 4x4; he tries to proposition her right there on the street, flinging down a bundle of Naira. Filmed in one tracking sequence, this shot has an unusual realism; in the background some fans watch the action from the balcony of their flat.

On the release of this film, Geneviève Nnaji (25 years old at the time) became the most highly paid actress in Nigeria (up to US$ 23,000 per role), and a superstar.

Jim Iyke, the male lead, is particularly good in his role as the Nigerian 'gangsta-rapper', just released from a spell in prison in the US (which had been 'a scandalous miscarriage of justice', according to the character's mother). The same year, Iyke joined the inner circle of the 'Big Six' – the most sought-after actors in the country.

Jealous Lovers is the only Nigerian film to have been put forward in the video category during FESPACO (the Pan-African Film Festival of Ouagadougou), 2005.

Date of release: 2003
Production/distribution: Cecilian Pictures/Videofield
Filmscript: Adim Williams
Cast: Geneviève Nnaji, Pat Attah, Jim Iyke & Florence Onouma.
Dialogue in English

9 Hausa Video & Sharia Law
Frédéric Noy

Kaduna city is clothed in a fine dust, like a fog, but even this can't deaden the sounds of clapping, as the Hausa Awards, the Oscars of Northern Nigeria, are being announced this evening. The elite of the profession have turned out. There is a bustling scene of traffic jams and beeping horns outside the gates of the venue. Actors are directing the traffic and deciding who comes through. Behind the gate is a rickety platform and a sea of plastic chairs. The wind flaps the cloth hanging up at the back, a translucent screen where the faces of the nominees billow about. The litany of prizes, punctuated by the appreciative applause of the mainly male audience, is greeted with exclamations from the women sitting in the shade. All the leading actresses are here, perched on their heels, sheathed in their gowns, playing to the smiles and glances of the men. The tension is palpable. Gathered together in the equivalent of the pit at the theatre they are all waiting for the announcement of the ultimate prize – Best Actress. The master of ceremonies tears open the envelope. One name cuts through the night air: 'Farida Jalal'. Ullulations and cries of joy accompany a fragile-looking 20-year-old as she climbs the steps. Falling to her knees to receive her second prize of the evening, Farida reflects on the journey she has made to reach this point. Two years previously she was begging producers to give her a break in their films. Since then there have been 25 other parts, fame, money and finally now the dream has come true. Yet by the following July her marriage sounds the end of her career:

> Being an actress is my life. My fans shower me with presents, but I am giving up everything for love. In any case, my husband would never agree to me carrying on being an actress. It is just not possible in our culture as a married woman.

Meanwhile, swept off by her kith and kin to avoid the crowds, she steps into a car which carries her off in a cloud of dust towards Kano. This Muslim, mainly Hausa city is a metropolis of 3 million people, situated 200 km to the north. Hausa is the largest ethnic group in Nigeria, representing almost 30 per cent of its 140 million inhabitants).

Its eroded earth ramparts (on which goats graze, feeding more often on plastic bags than on grass) still shelters its Emir's palace. Yet Kaduna is unaware of the fact that for the last 10 years, despite the return of Sharia law, it has become the mecca for film in the North of Nigeria.

Farida Jalal came here to look for her first role in film. like many young debutantes. However, according to some women here, actresses have never had good press in this conservative society. According to Mama Ajjo, a 43-year-old actress, this is because, 'in the 1980s, it was inconceivable that a woman should act in a television soap-opera, so the producers employed prostitutes.'

Today the low wages of these bar girls are just a memory. And the public want something new: they are tired of watching television broadcasts of Indian films that they don't understand. The democratization of video production and the unemployment among young people eager to create their own livelihoods, have all helped to give rise to the new business of home-video. It taps into a large source of money, propelling Nigeria up alongside the likes of Bollywood and Hollywood in the number of films produced.

Nigerian films shot, edited and duplicated on video, rarely screened in public, are blighted by technical errors. In this universe, two different worlds co-exist. Lagos and Onitsha/Aba, the southern cities, with Christian majorities, produce the largest proportion of the films, and Kano, the northern and Islamic outpost, dubbed 'Kanollywood' turns out 150 films each year.

The history of Kanollywood is rooted in Hausa romantic literature called *Soyayya* (meaning love), primarily written by women. Hajiya Balaraba Ramat, the Barbara Cartland of *Soyayya* remembers:

> I wrote a book called *Al Hakki* [Injustice]. In 1995 I met a director who wanted to adapt the story to film. I sold him the rights for 20,000 Naira (US$ 150). A miserable sum ... If I stood in his shoes I told myself, I could produce my own films, adapting my own novels and really make some money.

And so the movement was launched.

Today, the average budget for a film is as much as 500,000 Naira (US$ 3,800) excluding distribution. The fees earned by a top actress are in the region of 400,000 Naira (US$ 300) for five to six days work – this is in a city where 65 per cent of the inhabitants live on US$1 per day. 'The most difficult thing is to put together the money for the first film,' admits Umma Ali, President of the Women Executive Producers Association (WEPA) which has 20 members:

> Most of the producers are married and run small businesses. They sell jewellery, bags, shoes ... and economize Naira by Naira. That is the way I managed to make the first of these films ever produced by a woman, *Kadora Turga Pata*. That was in 1998!

Once a film has been edited, the producer gives the master, first-generation prints to the managers of the video-shops, who do the distribution. They also sell them the box-covers for 45 Naira each (US 35 cents). The distributor then copies the tapes, selling them on at 250 Naira each (US$ 1.9). There are 2,000 of these retail outlets covering Northern Nigeria, with a network in even the smallest market towns.

But there were some difficult times. In 2002, the market collapsed. There were too many films on the market, of too low a quality and from too many pseudo-producers. Of the 257 operators officially registered in Kano, only 60 of these were real producers, and among these, barely a dozen were women. Hajiya Balaraba Ramat offers an explanation:

> Women producers are vulnerable in Kano. They are mainly married, and tradition keeps them at home. They can't go out to negotiate prices, deal with their business affairs, or collect in money from their distributors. We are both economically dependant and exploited.

From this semi-seclusion they have to 'sub-contract' out to directors who happily swindle them out of their money. For this reason, the budgets on films produced by women are often twice as high as those made by men. Gradually, these women, whose stories and resources have contributed to the advent of home-video are disengaging from the business, waiting for more favourable times. However, a core group of professionals keeps going.

Tijjani Ibrahim is one of these. A young producer, 29 years old, originally from Maiduguri, she set up AMART Entertainment at the end of 2002. Pulling together a tiny budget, she produced the film *Ta Bayyana* for 900,000 Naira (less than US$ 7,000). It tells the story of Farida, an illegitimate girl who goes looking for her parents. Until now, Tijjani Ibrahim has only recuperated two-thirds of her investment, but despite this, thanks to other outside funding, she has managed to produce *Ta Bayyana II*, in which the heroine finds her parents. Farida is unable to marry Ahmed until she is rid of the blemish of illegitimacy. She drags her parents before an Islamic tribunal, which punishes them each with 100 lashes with a cane. Tijjani lets slip a smile: 'Illegitimacy is the parents' sin, not the child's. I believe in Sharia law. It is better to be punished on earth by men who follow God's law, than to be punished in heaven by God himself.'

Meanwhile, this budding director is sifting through technical advertisements for the latest models of video equipment that she wants for setting up AMART in Kano. She is optimistic about the future. Sales in 2003 went back up to their previous levels. American productions are barely shown in the country any more, Indian films still vie with Hausa films for a share of the market, but the situation is stabilizing. To make her mark on the industry, Tijjani would like to work with the new wave of directors who are real professionals, more in touch with their audiences. Such people come from a background similar to her own, have grown up immersed in Indian films (often regarded as too 'Bollywood' by the old guard producers and Hausa intellectuals), and are the ones whom the khadis dream of silencing with fatwas because their choreography and sound-tracks put beautiful actresses and the young male leads into close proximity. In Kano the fracture lines do not run between those who are pro- and anti-home-video, but between the old and the young. 'It is a generation gap,' Tijjani sums up cheerfully.

But how important is the opposition, when 70 per cent of the audiences are made up of women who are passionately fond of both the songs that their children hum in the back yards, and of the stories portrayed in the scripts: forced marriages, threatened romances, marital conflict, split loyalties between filial obedience and personal desire. These stories describe situations that everyone is familiar with, and their outcomes give the audience practical guidance for living their own lives. As the actress Ummu Al Amary remembers: 'I was out shopping one day when a woman came up to me and said that the role I had played in *Urmani*, was the story of her first marriage.'

The influence of Hausa films doesn't stop there – the fashions, the way to tie a headscarf, the way to move, the romantic encounters between young people, even the vocabulary changes. 'In *Sansani*', says Farida Jalal, 'my character used Hausa slang. Some of these expressions have now been taken up by the young people of Kano.'

Even in neighbouring francophone Niger, to be 'cool' you have to speak Hausa with the accent taken from the Kano films. Diffusion of this kind operates across frontiers.

'Every week,' claims Idriss Dan Zaria, President Video Marketers Association of Kano, 'I send cars packed with hundreds of copies of the latest films to all the towns of Northern Nigeria. I even cover Niger!'

But even if Kano's output spreads out all around the Hausa hinterland, to perhaps more than 45 million people in Nigeria, Niger, Ghana, the Sudan, Cameroon and Benin, it has no interest at all in television. The derisory amount of money paid for the right to broadcast (1,500 Naira), is less than the income received from selling 33 tapes. And profit is the objective here.

The stars also count the zeros, but when they are struggling, it is often the prospect of a good marriage that motivates them, even more than wealth and fame. The actresses may be despised by ordinary men, but they are often courted by the more educated ones. The characters in their films speak for them. With their well-turned out appearance, their reputation of being at ease in society and their good looks, they watch suitors home in on them from afar, both geographically and socially. At the age of 22, didn't Maijidda Ibrahim, the much-admired actress, become the second wife of the son of the Emir of

A young actress rehearses a dance scene; Hausa films are heavily influenced by Indian cinema
(© Frédéric Noy)

Kano, the highest traditional and religious authority in the State? A Cinderella in 'Kanollywood': a social about-turn which changes the 'debauched' woman into a princess before whom fathers (who would previously turn their backs) now have to kneel.

The world of Hausa film is no longer a real contradiction. The seclusion of the wives works against the husbands. The films reach women cloistered in their houses by tradition, but at home they sway to the rhythm of the songs and dances that the religion publicly condemns. So home-video has set up an ambiguous relationship between itself and Hausa society. On the one hand, the local films portray negative aspects of what are seen as corrupt Southern Christian cultures, but on the other, if producers gave up on this popular art form its place would be taken by Indian films, or worse still, films from the South of Nigeria itself. Tolerated for a while by Sharia, by the year 2000, the government of Kano had suspended the licences of all of the film producers and distributors. Two years later a censorship law allowed them back into business. The law acknowledges, in effect, that to censor an art form is to recognize its existence. Since this judicial about-turn, producers need to have a permit from the National Film and Video Censors Board (NFVCB) to operate, and

Hausa actress Saratu Gidadu or 'Daso', here being directed on set, won the prize for 'best actress in the role of a villain' at the Yahoo Awards in Kano

(© Frédéric Noy)

they also need one from Kano State. Obsessed with keeping men and women apart publicly, the Kano State tried to issue a decree requiring directors to shoot musical scenes in two parts: first the men, then the women, finally re-uniting them in the editing. This attempt at control was greeted with sneers of derision by the profession. The decree was never implemented. The Board was reduced to censoring a scene because of a low-cut dress or for having breached the taboo on contact. Whether such scenes were edited out or not, the much valued distribution licence added 5,000 Naira (US$ 38) to all production budgets.

Alhaji Mohamed isn't bothered by all these formalities. Thursday evening is a special time for his family. One of his six sons has gone to the corner shop to rent a film for 20 Naira (US 15 cents). In the evenings there are few other distractions outside, as Sharia law forbids Muslims from going to the last few places left that have dancing and alcohol. Ceremoniously, just as in many other houses across the city, the eldest son comes back, turns on the television and the video machine. All eyes are fixed on the flickering image. While the nasal sound of the title music attracts the neighbours, Mohammed's wife settles down at the back of the room with her youngest in her arms.

Frédéric Noy

The noise of the generator, cutting in during the frequent and long-lasting power failures, drowns out some of the dialogue of *Sansani*, this latest film from FKD Production starring Farida Jalal. The film lasts an hour and a half and tells the story of two senior wives of a notable Muslim who vie for status in the house, then fight each other over the inheritance of their deceased husband's estate, and finally join forces against a younger third wife.

Elsewhere, under the guidance of Ali Nuhu, a well-respected director, a young female understudy is getting ready to go on set; a friend of Nuhu's wife had introduced 20-year-old Hauwa Mussa to the director. In the casting of 'Kanollywood' films, it is common for people to be co-opted from the director's social circle. There are no signs of anxiety on the face of this young divorcée on the threshold of her career, fluttering her eyelashes as she dismisses the memory of her family's disapproval when she told them that she wanted to be an actress: 'I am a good Muslim, not a prostitute. I know what I can do and what I can't!'

Behind her, the crew busy themselves in the director's living room, doubling as the set for this latest film. There are no studios in Kano, so people use each other's homes whenever possible. An electrician patches up an extension cable to two battered spotlights. The actresses listen as the director gives his last instructions. The make-up artist moves silently from one actor to the next with a heavy box of her silvery tools. The floodlights switch on. A crackling follows. An anxious glance from the director of photography (also cameraman) is picked up by one of the actors (also production manager). Will the bulb hold out? The director (also the lead actor) reads the look on the face of his brother, the assistant director (also the film's producer). Is there enough fuel for the generator in case there is a power cut? Action. The digital camera, cupped in the hands of the cameraman, looks quite fragile and the viewing screen that the director is scrutinizing is very small. The actors start up their dialogue. If the traffic isn't too heavy outside; the camera's microphone should pick up the essential bits. A shadow suddenly falls over the room. A power cut. As if in response, the muezzins begin their call to evening prayer above the rooftops of Kano.

Film Profile No. 9
Khusufi
Directed by Ali Nuhu

Habib and Khalid are the two adopted sons of Al Hadji Madu, a rich merchant from Kano. Their father's business takes them to Mecca where the young Arab girls waste no time flirting with them. On their return to Kano the two young men go back to their father's farm. Out walking in the bush, Khalid meets and falls in love with Hajjo, a young Fulani herder who dreams of becoming a singer. In order to seduce her, Khalid holds out the temptation of a brilliant career for her in the city.

Hajjo's father, Mallam, is resistant at first to his daughter's choice of career. He doesn't know about the existence of this suitor, but finally, under pressure from his circle of friends and neighbours, he relents and decides to go with Hajjo to Kano, in order to make the necessary contacts for her. His first visit is to a childhood acquaintance, who is none other than Al Hadji Madu. His friend is not at home: Mallam is very poorly received by the merchant's wife, a conceited middle-class woman who treats him like a dog. Beside himself with rage, Mallam calls her an 'old prostitute'. Despite the arrival of Al Hadji Madu, who recognizes his old companion from their childhood herding days, the quarrel becomes even more bitter and Mallam ends up hitting Madu. He storms out in a temper, taking Hajjo with him. Khalid is very unhappy to see his intended being swept away from him.

Despite this scene, Mallam doesn't give up on the project that brought him to Kano: the launch of his daughter's musical career. The first impresario that he contacts is surprisingly ethical, with an impeccable reputation for professionalism and integrity. (In any film from Southern Nigeria, this character would automatically have been a vicious adventurer ready to pounce on his prey.) Without hesitation he offers Hajjo an audition for the part of the female lead in a musical-comedy called *Khusufi*.

Gratified by his daughter's good fortune, old Mallam tells himself 'God is great'. Before he leaves Kano, Khalid visits him, all contrite, begs forgiveness and asks for his daughter's hand in marriage. The old Fulani generously agrees that Khalid can marry his daughter on

Date of release: 2003
Production/distribution: Ahmad Nuhu/FKD Productions
Filmscript: Ali Nuhu
Cast: Kabiru Nakwango, Ali Nuhu, Ahmad Nuhu, Rukayya Umar, Auwa Ali Dodo, Usaini Sule Koki & Maijidda Ibrahim
Dialogue in Hausa, with English sub-titles

Ali Nuhu, actor, writer, director and millionaire, at his wedding
(© Frédéric Noy)

one condition: he has to free himself from his father's domineering ways and live an independent life.

Without raising the subject of marriage, Khalid is able to convince his father that he should go his own way, whatever wealth Al Hadji Madu has amassed for he and his brother Habib to inherit. With his father's blessing, Khalid set out to find work, and by good fortune is immediately hired by a company in Kano.

Mallam returns to Al Hadji Madu's house, to the latter's great surprise. The audience is expecting a reconciliation, but in fact, the grudging Mallam assaults his childhood friend verbally with this lesson in truth: 'Well a dog has managed to do something that you were never capable of doing – make your son independent.'

Khusufi portrays the vibrancy of youth in a plot interspersed with musical clips that are not without charm. The scenes located in Saudi Arabia seem a bit gratuitous, but the same could be said for the London scenes of various films from Southern Nigeria. Clearly directors and audiences can't resist the fascination of wealth, the city of London being a kind of Mecca for Nigerians from the coast. The Saudi interlude does however provide some dead-pan comic scenes involving a sensitive servant who is deaf. The technical limitations of the camera-work – clearly shot with an amateur digital camera set on automatic exposure – are made up for with skilful editing and by music that is repetitive but does have charm.

Film Profile No. 10
The Lost Honour of Maryam Usman
Directed by Usman Bobo

Date of release: July 2007
Directed by: Usman Bobo &
Maryam Usman
Cast: Usman Bobo & Maryam
Usman (of *Hiyana* fame)
Length: 8 minutes

It is early 2006 in a Lagos apartment and a time when Maryam Usman was not the Hausa superstar that she became after the release of the films *Kambun So*, *Habafin So*, *Aska* and *Hiyana*, produced by Ali Nuhu. However, the film made that day meant that her other work was disregarded. It wasn't distributed until a year and a half after the 'filming', but it gave Maryam a celebrity status beyond that of her other films and at the same time not only ruined her career but put the whole Hausa film industry into disrepute.

Back in Lagos, the setting is the apartment of Maryam's lover, a certain Usman Bobo, who usually runs a bureau de change and has probably never handled a real camera. Using his mobile phone, he films Maryam stretched out on the bed, completely naked but covered with a sheet. Then he gives the phone to Maryam so that she can also film him strolling naked around the flat. After making an exhibition of himself in this way, he takes the phone back from her and the end of the recording is so frenetic that it is hard to make out exactly what is happening, but Bobo is clearly trying to film a sexual encounter with Maryam that records their foreplay but not the act of inter-course itself.

In July 2007, by which time Maryam has become the most popular actress that the Hausa film industry had ever known, Bobo's video started to circulate by mobile phone, CD, video and memory stick. Later on Maryam was to accuse other Hausa actressses of having been among the first to sell copies of the film at US$10 each. The video was then put on line through blogs and other internet sites.

The scandal was such that professionals in the Hausa film industry immediately realized the potential damage this could do to their work. Hoping to appease the censors they took a series of preventitive measures themselves as damage limitation: they suspended production, imposed sanctions on Maryam (a five-year ban on working in the industry) and on about twenty others including some of the most popular actresses such as Farida Jalal and Safiya Musa. The latter, at the time of the hearing, continued to dress in the 'indecent' way that she had been reproached for: 'I don't care what these people think ... I will dress how I like. I have a suitcase full of T-shirts, mini T-shirts and short skirts.'[1]

But their attempts to clean up didn't succeed in calming the champions of Sharia law. Actresses were harrassed and intimidated and their cars were burned. The Censorship Board in Kano adopted a series of new restrictive measures: a procedure of registering and licensing concessions for all professionals in the industry, a filing and censoring of screenplays, and a monitoring of the film shoots and locations. Fortified by these new means of controlling the industry, in February 2008 they authorized that filming could start again. But the supporters of Sharia law remained unappeased by these efforts. On the 22 March 2008, the actress Zainab Umar was arrested and detained for more than 24 hours by Hisbah, Kano's pro-Sharia militia. Several directors were arrested and fined for releasing allegedly uncensored films.

In sum, the 'Hiyana' affair as it is known, has unsettled the whole of the Hausa film industry. As to Maryam Usman, her career seems to be completely over. In November 2007 she married her long-time suitor Ado Dangulla. In keeping with Hausa tradition it is likely that as a married woman her career would be at an end anyway, with or without the Bobo video.

Film Profile No. 10
The Lost Honour
of Maryam Usman

1. Interview given in *Afrique Echos*, 23 November 2007.

10 Spielberg & I: The Digital Revolution[1]
Tunde Kelani

For almost fifty years, Nigeria's contribution to third world cinema was nothing to write home about. In just a decade, the growth due to the incursion of video productions has produced a phenomenon that has intrigued scholars, journalists, researchers and other experts in an attempt to reveal this Nigerian magic. The industry with all its flaws, according to the *New York Times* has been estimated at about US$ 35 million[2] annually: revenue that is funded only by private enterprise.

No wonder all the spotlights are on the Nigerian model. But today, we stand at a technological crossroads. In case you missed *Artsville* published 1 June 2003, I shall reproduce a few lines just to kick off the debate.

Tunde Kelani and Steven Spielberg should sit down and talk. On the future of film distribution, the two men are diametrically opposed. Nigeria's most acknowledged movie producer holds the view that digital production and distribution is the only way to succeed, especially if you are operating in the third world. 'Not exactly,' says Spielberg, the world's most acclaimed director. 'I am a Luddite', a recent edition of the British weekly *The Economist* quotes him as saying. Spielberg, who is credited with such hits as *Jaws, Saving Private Ryan* and *Schindler's List*, is a romantic who believes that the digital moving image robs movie-making of its artistry. He makes lavish use of computer-generated special effects but he still passionately prefers the look and feel of a celluloid.

[handwritten margin note: digital vs film]

The above piece is useful to quote because here in Nigeria some of our diehards in private and government circles support Spielberg's views. My disposition is guided by my professional experience having successfully worked in both media. I have shot enough celluloid, starting from my early television days, to stretch from Lagos to Sokoto and back. I could also be as passionate about the look and feel of celluloid if I had access to US $50 million, the average Hollywood budget for a film. But reality and experience have conditioned me to think differently.

The Naira to dollar exchange during the Structural Adjustment Programme years was probably 85:1. Today, the Naira exchanges for almost 140: 1. Yet shooting in celluloid relies heavily on foreign

1. The original version of this article appeared under the title 'Technological crossroads' in the Independent Television Producers Association of Nigeria, bulletin *ITPAN News*, volume 2, no. 5, published in July 2003 at the occasion of the third 'Lagos Film Forum', supported by the French Embassy in Nigeria.
2. The estimated figure given by the National Film and Video Censors Board 2003 is in excess of US$ 80 million.

production facilities and services available abroad and payable in foreign currency. Nobody is willing to put down any kind of fund for such projects just to prove a point.

How do we utilize the available resources and source funds to make high quality films? Inevitably, I started the shift towards an alternative technology which provides answers to the expensive and rather exclusive celluloid based filmmaking especially in developing nations like Nigeria.

The assertion that the only way we could produce quality films is by shooting celluloid is just not true. As a matter of priority, I simply suggest that we start looking at the digital alternative to filmmaking which has had some astounding successes within the last few years. Let me give you a few examples. At the top, is George Lucas' *Phantom Menace*, shot entirely digitally. I had the privilege of watching this blockbuster at the Odeon, Leicester Square Cinema – the traditional home of the *Star Wars* series – to experience what digital film would be like. George Lucas, an equal to Spielberg in the technological context, cheekily faded on the first opening graphics 'This film was shot digitally', to rub it in. I believed I had watched a 35mm celluloid projected copy, having visited Bucks Film laboratory in the UK and been given the privileged information that 800 copies of 35mm of *The Phantom Menace* had been scanned from digital to negative and printed for cinema release throughout the UK. This makes economic sense since all the mechanical projectors installed in the theatres are still running efficiently. (In Nigeria, there is not a single decent 35mm projector working reliably and consistently today.)[3] Anyway, I was shocked when I picked the *Evening Standard* review of *Phantom Menace* to discover in an article titled 'The end of the reel', that the version I had watched at the Odeon, Leicester Square, was indeed digitally projected. The experience for me, especially in sound reproduction, was unbelievable. I quickly consoled myself that such quality in picture and sound was only possible digitally with the high-end digital video, High Definition, which again will be prohibitively costly for struggling filmmakers in Africa.

Is it possible for high quality films to be made digitally with low-cost equipment It is, of course, and there are some surprising success stories. First of the list of films that caught my attention was the winner of Camera d'Or at the Cannes 2001 film festival. *Atarnajuat*, by a first time director Zacharias Kunuk, was shot digitally with Sony DSR 500 and transferred to film at Swiss Effects Studios in Zürich. There are probably many DSR 500 camcorders lying idle in Nigeria. And who has not heard of the *Blair Witch Project*, a mere US$ 30,000–50,000 film shot with small digital video camcorders and marketed using the awesome powers and reach of the internet.

While we are at it, Ellen Kuras ASC, a brilliant cinematographer earned the Excellence award at the 2002 Sundance Film Festival for

3. Written in 2003. This is no longer the case in 2008. Lagos has more than a dozen modern cinemas equipped with 35mm projectors.

the film *Personal Velocity*. You guessed right, the film was shot on digital video with Sony DSR PD 150 pro-super camcorder costing about US$ 4,000. Apart from her other prestigious awards, she was also the first to win the award for a project that did not originate on film.

I have been kicking myself ever since. Perhaps we should begin a process of technical re-orientation before we lose our way completely. The digital revolution if embraced could help us to overcome the divide between us and the developed nations. I certainly do not miss the bulky reels of 35mm print and the mechanical monstrosity called the 35mm projecter. Just give me my 3,000 lumen projector and my film burned from my timeline to DVD.

During my last miserable experience of screening *Iwa*, a 16mm film which I co-produced, there was a technical hitch with the projector at the National Theatre, Lagos. By the time we hurried to the projection booth upstairs, 900ft had been destroyed beyond repair. Today, all I need to do is re-write another copy of the DVD, same quality. I looked on open-mouthed at the variety of digital projection presentations at NAB, Las Vegas, two years ago on giant screens playing back not on film or DVD but computer servers. With US$ 75,000, I could come up with a digital laboratory equivalent to our Jos elephantine project complete with digital sound dubbing studios that can mix 5.1 surround sound.

And who has not already heard of sending high-quality non-compressed digital video and audio down broadband width up and down the internet? We should make sure we are never left that far behind again.

Since our cinematic infrastructure has already collapsed, we have an opportunity to rebuild from scratch. The new cinemas will probably be smaller, decent, equipped with digital projectors playing from digital media with digital Surround 5.1 sound making the cinematic experience worthwhile.

Film Profile No. 11
Agogo Eewo
Directed by Tunde Kelani

Agogo Eewo is the second part of a trilogy following *Saworoide*, the story of a Yoruba village ruled by a tyrannical petty-king. In the earlier episode (inspired by the era of the murderous Sani Abacha, who 'ruled' or rather, as some say, 'dismembered' Nigeria from 1994 to 1998), the story unfolds of an enlightened king who is approached while working at his farm and asked whether he would put his wisdom and impartiality to the service of the community. Despite his own integrity, he has to rule with an entourage of corrupt and scheming traditional elders. This fable is inspired by the re-establishment of democracy in Nigeria and election of Olusegun Obasanjo to the presidency. He was returned to power twenty years after giving up power to a civilian government in 1979.

The second part, *Agogo Eewo*, filmed in Abeokuta, is remarkable for the magnificence of its sets, costume and lighting. The influence of Yoruba travelling theatre is apparent in many scenes, and for the most part tastefully done. The film suffers from a predictable ending, with the wicked being victims of their own ill-doings.

Since its release, *Agogo Eewo*, has been embroiled in a running dispute between its creator – largely supported by professional Nigerians – and the National Film and Video Censors Board (NFVCB) who classified the film as 'unsuitable for under-18s', although there isn't a single scene that is particularly violent or shocking. In the first volume of its *Film and Video Directory* (2003), the NFVCB devoted one paragraph to the justification of its position with regard to this work:

> The film has been classified as '18' (Adult) because the Board considers that *Agogo Eewo* contains an excessive amount of fetishist practice, violence, corruption, seduction, etc., which are not suitable for children. Because of the prolific use of 'gris-gris', fetishist rituals, violence and sex in Nigerian films, and a lack of variety in their plots, the Board wanted to discourage a repetition of these themes.[1]

Nearly two years later, Tunde Kelani recalled this event:

> How could they say that my film *Agogo Eewo* was fetishist? Someone

Date of release: 2002
Production: Mainframe
Filmscript: Akinwunmi Isola
Editing: Wale Kelani
Set: Pat Nebo
Cast: Dejumo Lewis, Lere Paimo, Larinde Akinleye, Adebayo Faleti, Deola Faleye, Kayode Olaiya
Dialogue in Yoruba, sub-titled in English

1. This paragraph features in a chapter entitled 'Producers of Obscene Films Told to Watch Out'. Applying the term 'obscene' to a film by Tunde Kelani is really perplexing. Referred to usually as 'TK', he is one of the rare Nigerian directors to have been considered as a real filmmaker, in both his own country and abroad, because of both the artistic quality of his films and their moral and philosophical significance.

Film Profile No. 11
Agogo Eewo

who is heading up a Board of Censors such as ours ought to have sufficient understanding of things relating to African culture, lifestyles, roots, values and modes of expression. Ignorance about our own culture is really a kind of alienation. For example, the 'gong' which symbolizes communication, if you didn't understand its purpose, you might call it a 'fetish'.[2]

2. Cited from the *Nollywood* supplement to *New Age*, 10 September 2004.

Despite being banned from television broadcast, *Agogo Eewo* was a big hit with the public, selling more than 100,000 copies.

Opposite: Video shop in Lagos

(© Robert Minangoy)

PART II
Nollywood & its Conquest of Africa

11 Niger & Nollywood: The New Romantics
Ibbo Daddy Abdoulaye

Niamey, end of October, 8pm. Talladje is slowly waking up. In this suburb on the outskirts of the city, the streets are giving off a strong smell of spices as at the end of every day during Ramadan; grilled meat and mint tea. Built leaning against the wall of a house is a pocket-sized video shop lit by a bare lamp. As usual a small crowd of inquisitive children and adults forms an animated queue.

In this small shop, packed to bursting, the people are indifferent to the distant sounds of a sermon being broadcast through a loud-speaker. They are crammed in like sardines, eyes fixed on an old colour television which is showing a Hausa video-film.

The screen shows familiar scenes, easily mistaken for an Indian film apart from the nationality of the actors and the language spoken. By the finale, after two hours of singing, dancing, intrigues, domestic scenes, disputes and recriminations, the anti-hero has been punished for all his wrong-doings and the orphan child has become a beautiful girl, married to the prince of her dreams.

However trivial this kind of story can be, the people of Niger can't seem to get enough of them. Owning a video player is no longer a means of showing off to the outside world. These days it is the essential tool for any father who wants to keep his children at home. In the city as in the rural areas low-paid people go to neighbours' houses or to one of the numerous video-clubs that have sprung up everywhere. For just FCFA 25–50 (5–10 US cents) entry fee, these clubs present *Dandalin Soyyaya*, the name given to the Nigerian films based on romantic novels. This bit of equipment has become so central to the way of life that a young girl might ask her fiancé to buy one for her as part of a bride-price. The explanation is simple: she needs to make sure that married life is not going to interrupt her daily intake of *Dandalin Soyyaya*.

How many are there ... 1,000, 10,000 or 100,000 of these films? 'Only God knows exactly how many Nigerian video-cassettes are currently circulating in Niger', says Issaka Doulla, who treats the question as if he had been asked how many stars are in the sky. When pushed for an answer, this trader from Niamey's Grand

Recording a musical soundtrack in Kano. In Hausa video, as in Indian cinema, the score at times conveys more than the visuals

(© Frédéric Noy)

Marché, who advertises his latest arrivals on television and radio, confirms that he receives 'at least 500 new cassettes and CDs each week'. The reason for the absence of statistics is twofold. Firstly, the majority of those dealing in video-cassettes do so through the informal sector and so are not regulated in any way. According to Issaka Doulla there are thousands like him across the country. Secondly, the border between Niger and Nigeria is long (1,500km) and porous, and all kinds of traffickers dealing in video-cassettes have no problem crossing this line and flooding the market with these highly desirable products. A customs officer at the Dan Issa border post in Maradi describes how difficult it is to monitor the trade:

> Everyone who goes regularly to Nigeria comes back with two to three *Dandalin Soyyaya* cassettes – especially at this time of year during Ramadan when people want to distract themselves from hunger by consuming films that are Halal.

Hadjia Dellou from Maradi who trades in cloth and utensils and regularly makes the trip between the two countries offers slightly more convincing evidence:

> Each trip I make, people are asking me to bring the latest films. We often give cassettes to the customs officers as presents, to sweeten them up so that they turn a blind eye.

These are just different ways to avoid the regulations and to get around declaring the full quantity of cassettes in case they are taxed at customs.

Whether it is smuggling on a large or a small scale, the effect is that thousands of cassettes seep across the border. Transporting them is difficult, but it can bring in a large income to those who use this trade as their lifeline. Zakary Jady, a young graduate from Niger, could not find work so threw himself into the very profitable business of renting out video-cassettes and V-CDs of mainly Nigerian films. He makes 'FCFA 250–500 a day (50 cents–US$ 1) for each cassette or V-CD, depending on the client, plus the fines which are a fee for each day they are returned late. Renting gives him a profit of FCFA 5,000-10,000 (US$ 10–20), before the cassette is worn out. In contrast, selling a cassette or V-CD rarely brings in more than FCFA 1,000.

The big hits of these low-cost films, such as *Wassila, Sangaya, Tubali, Ki Yarda Da Ni, Sa'adatu Sa'a Maata*, are mostly rented out to women, who know all the actors' dialogues by heart. There is even a flourishing business in making audio-cassette copies of the songs; these are played again and again throughout the day on radio stations, in taxis, in hair-dressing salons and in most other public places.

People are often better informed about the smallest actions and gestures of the stars of these films than larger questions of national interest, thanks to all the posters pasted over walls, and because of Hausa language fan magazines such as *Fina Fina* or *Dunyar Fim*. Some enterprising types have spotted a good opportunity and turn up as impersonators of the stars, performing for small change at baptism and weddings. There are also groups who perform, more professionally, the complete repertoires of the much-adored film music and songs.

The success of these films from Kano, Kaduna, Jos and Ibadan is such that the Brazilian and Mexican series that previously dominated television broadcasting, have been pushed aside. A drop in the popularity and audiences figures caused a quick reaction from Channel 2, Tal TV, aimed at the youth market. It has tried to correct the trend and has gone back to programming Nigerian videos[1] to the great joy of the television viewers as well as to some of those who rent out the cassettes. 'At first', says Zakary Jady, 'I thought that television would kill my business.' But far from destroying it, by broadcasting these

1. Using the term *'navet'* (flop) is fully justified for some Hausa films whose quality is very poor. The film *Sayen Baki*, screened in October 2003 at the Marhaba cinema in Kano was so bad that the audience left the cinema in droves. Apart from its technical faults, the films dragged out a story for nearly two hours that could have been dealt with in 20 minutes. *Gamji*, produced by the choreographer John Flash Stephen, is also tiresome for its length and the naivety of its plot, although the set and style of production had some interesting aspects. However, some Hausa films stand out from the rest and are of a quality that matches that of the Southern Nigerian films. Examples of this are Hafizu Bello's *Ruhi* and films by the brothers Ali and Ahmad Nuhu.

films, television has become the best way to promote them and to promote video-rental.' As Zakary explains, 'the women who had missed the film on television hurry to rent it and even those who had seen it want to watch it again, when they are more relaxed, often with their husbands.'

In contrast to those who rent out videos, the people who sell them are less happy as their sales drop because of television broadcasts. One of them even threatened to take the national television station before the Author's Copyright Society for 'broadcasting cinematic productions without the necessary authorization of the author and without having paid any copyright fees...'

The threat was taken seriously by the directors of Tal-TV: 'Our first reaction was to stop broadcasting these films,' explained Sani Ousmane, the channel's programme director. 'But the interruption didn't last long because the managers of Tal-TV were sent an avalanche of insulting letters, especially from television viewers who could not understand why the broadcast of such films, which had successfully won back an audience to public television, should be stopped in its tracks.'

As soon as it could, the channel tried to get a green light from the copyright-holders in Nigeria. 'Something that wasn't very easy as anyone who knows the communication problems with the country will understand.' Then they turned to the Nigerian Embassy in Niamey 'to find out about the current legislation on the subject' in relation to their southern neighbour. The response from the television company's side was positive on two counts. They confirmed that thanks to 'Ibro Ben Laden', a Nigerian actor who is very well-known in Niamey, 'we were able to make telephone contact with one of Nigeria's established film producers in Kano; he judged the reaction of his colleagues in Niger to be ill-considered, and assured us of his support.' Sani Ousmane added that the Cultural Attaché at the Nigerian Embassy was more than pleased with the cultural exposure that the films were giving his country, and was not inclined to back any proceedings against the broadcasters.

Since then, the television audiences have been happier, and the director of Tal-TV recalls: 'You should have seen the number of women who came each day to congratulate us.' He does not see the broadcasting of these films as a foreign influence; quite the opposite. For him 'Niger is the same as Nigeria, they are like Hassane and Ousseini (names usually given to twin brothers). What's the problem when we have the same culture, the same religion and when, quite often, even the stories are drawn from our own repertoire?'

This is exactly what hurts, retorts Souleymane Sanda, stage director, producer, film director and head of the theatrical troupe 'Amadou Dan Bassa' (which later became 'Yazi Dogo'). Between 1980 and 1995 they were involved in most of the theatrical productions that were shown on radio and national television. He remembers their heyday when they were doing up to 'four productions a month', and complains about the sloppiness of the younger generation: 'Our young artist brothers have become lazy – the *Dandalin Soyyaya* films are nothing but pale imitations of the *Wassan Fague* of the old days.' In his opinion even the revenue that is earned from these successful films is not hard to explain: 'There is no technical expertise here; the shots aren't set up; there are only long uncut sequences. So what's the problem?' he asks (apart from the fact that the government doesn't do anything about promoting the culture of Niger itself). 'We used to be the best in Africa at both theatre and film' he says, with a surge of quite proper national pride, 'and now we are the worst'. 'Why are the people of Niger becoming just consumers of other basically Hausa cultures?' and adds that 'the main thing that women like in these films are the songs.' Ironically, most of these songs are drawn from Niger's culture. 'It's just that the people here don't realise this', Sanda points out, angry with the passive attitude of the government which according to him has an aversion to 'culture'.

Niger's culture is so rich and the plot of so many of the Nigerian films so weak, but somehow people's eyes and ears are only tuned in to the latter. Elhadji Issoufou Mamane deplores the fact that 'People from Niger only like to consume things from abroad and disdain things that are produced locally. All the films that are valued today wouldn't have the same appeal if they were made by us.' This radio presenter was one of the people who contributed to the success of Nigerian films with his programme *Dandalin Soyayya*, which first introduced to the audiences of Niger the themes of these films.

What is the impact of these films on the public, and especially on the young, who clearly have a thirst for them? Opinions differ about this. Mahamadou Alio, a computer buff who watches two videos a day with his family, says 'It's simple, I only bring home cassettes that are stamped with the seal of the Nigerian Censors Board.' Another, with a serious expression, explains that he has noticed 'positive changes' in the behaviour of his wife 'since she has been watching the films, the ones based on the Hadiths of the prophet.' A third gave the following explanation:

> We live in a society where, whatever mistakes our elders or parents make, it is not possible to point these out to them directly ... So all you have to do is to put on a film that is against these things and then they understand and change the way they behave ... It's the same thing with our folk tales, there is always a moral behind them.

Ibbo Daddy Abdoulaye

One fifty-year-old taxi driver insisted on recounting the story of his passage from 'dream to reality'. Captivated by the behaviour of the women in Hausa films, he married a woman from Kano. Thanks to a cinematic flow of ideas, Niger is in the process of changing its habits. These films are distributed without sub-titles, yet even those who can't hold a real conversation in Hausa, are devotees.

'I watch the film and then I explain the story to my neighbours,' says one indecisive customer, looking through a pile of cassettes. 'And it's a great way to improve my Hausa,' she says, with a roar of laughter that exposes her gold tooth.

Partly due to these films, the use of Hausa has spread into most households. So will Hausa become, in the future, the common language of Niger's different ethnic groups? This question doesn't perturb Zakary Jady:

> When I first started out there were a couple of civil servants who used to come to take out videos. Early on, only the wife would get out of their car, and while she was choosing, the husband, who didn't speak a word of the language would just get impatient and sound his horn, cursing Hausa films which he didn't think much of at all. These days, curiously, it is her husband who comes in to choose the films.

It is a strange rebuttal to all those at the 1991 National Conference in who were opposed to the adoption of Hausa as the national language. Boubacar Issa Bagalam, born in Maradi, isn't someone who defends the value system portrayed in these films, but admits without hesitation 'that the cultural influence of Nigeria is very evident. But I would rather my children were influenced by Nigerian culture than by the trash in Brazilian soaps.'

Other people have a problem with the Hausa films, such as Abdoul-razak Hallilou, who points the finger at

> some of the behaviour which is completely alien to our culture, such as giving flowers to a woman, or a man dancing to court a woman, or even climbing up the wall of a house to sneak into a woman's bedroom.

Paradoxically, while Niger is doing its utmost to copy the films coming from its southern neighbour, the Nigerians are moving in the opposite direction: Kaduna State television sent a man to Niger television to negotiate for copies of all the popular songs and theatre productions that are available. Sani Ousmane is not surprised by this: 'The context is the same.' He even sees 'an excellent opportunity for multi-culturalism'. Others fear that such dependence will lead to a loss of Niger's own cultural identity. In the Hausa departments of the many radio stations in Niamey, people are expected to speak Hausa with a Nigerian accent. And no Hausa presenter is taken seriously unless they pepper their speech with Nigerian or 'British' expressions.

It is 'chic' to speak the same Hausa as the actors in *Dandallin Soyayya*, even if the listeners are taken by surprise.

*V-CD cover of
Izu Ojukwu's
Sitanda*

Film Profile No. 12
Sitanda
Directed by Izu Ojukwu

The character played by Stephanie Okereke is humiliated by a merciless husband who complains bitterly about everything she does – including, worst of all, her poor cooking. In despair, she goes home to her parents' village. One of her husband's harsh remarks not only hurt her, but also intrigued her, as she doesn't understand why he called her a 'pariah'. Her father explains the word in the form of a long flashback about her ancestor Sitanda who had been banished by his tribe after having been reduced to slavery. The scene changes to Africa in pre-colonial times, where the young Sitanda was brought up by an old man, his guardian. The boy gets involved with a group of slaves amongst whom he soon spots the young and beautiful Azizat.

Over-run with anachronistic declarations of passion, the film combines a love-story with a warrior's adventures. We learn that Sitanda is the queen's son and that he was taken away at birth. Unknown to his mother, a man who had ambitions to usurp her plotted to put a female baby in the young heir's place. The secret of Sitanda's birth is revealed after the death of the king, poisoned by the same usurper. Eventually, the pretender is unmasked. The old slave Sitanda is therefore called to the throne, but at the same time, his beloved Azizat is chosen to join a group of young girls condemned to be sacrificed at the king's funeral. To save his sweetheart, Sitanda must renounce the throne and run away with her. In this way, the couple and all their descendants all become pariahs.

Sitanda is a production of Amstel Box Office, a subsidiary of the company that distributes Dutch beer. It sponsors one of the leading TV-reality shows on Nigerian television. The creator of *Sitanda*, Izu Ojukwu, is one of the rare Nigerian video directors to have received his training in cinema. In fact he took a course at the Jos National Film Insitute, an under-funded and very badly equipped film school that still succeeds in producing very talented and well-educated trainee film directors. The film *Sitanda* is of an artistic standard that the home-video audience rarely sees. Two scenes of particular quality come to mind: first, the introductory sequence where Stephanie Okereke, victimized by her husband, has to return home in torrential

Date of release: 2007
Production: Amstel Box Office
Cast: Stephanie Okereke, Ali Nuhu, Ireti Doyle & Azizat Sadiq
Winner of the best production in the African Movie Academy Awards, 2007

Film Profile No. 12
Sitanda

rain. This brilliantly poignant episode is so full of promise that the rest of the film is a huge disappointment: banal in every way. However, there is one gripping scene still to come, depicting a raid by Arab horsemen. The scene is surprising because this kind of historical episode is rarely depicted in sub-Saharan Africa, and also because it relates to a current situation, exposed in the international media, but never portrayed visually: the terrifying mounted Janjawid who have brought fire and blood to the Darfur region of Sudan. Even here, with this sequence, there is an unexpected flash of brilliance that lifts the film above its banal storyline. Otherwise the narrative is rather formulaic and as if carefully meeting a 'federalist', if not frankly 'federal' agenda.

The casting was clearly more important than the plot, bringing together – very unusually for a Nigerian film – the superstar of the South, Stephanie Okereke, the most sought-after young lead from Hausa films, Ali Nuhu, and the rising star Azizat Sadiq, whose career was launched in a television programme of which *Sitanda* is really a derivative. In this respect the film illustrates the growing tendency in Nigerian home-video to give in, not only to the demands of the promoters and marketers of the V-CD market, but also to commercial companies, churches of every persuasion, and awareness-raising programmes (for example in the fight against Aids) – all of which are using the popularity of home-video to get their message out. The worry is that this tendency to graft social messages or large publicity campaigns onto the films will lead Nollywood to lose if not its 'soul', then certainly its unique identity.

12 Kinshasa & Nollywood: Chasing the Devil
Franck Baku Fuita & Godefroid Bwiti Lumisa

◄◄

After a two-year period in which there was a flurry of broadcasting Nigerian films in the Democratic Republic of Congo (DRC), the Minister of Information and Media decided to call a halt. In March 2003, Nigerian films were banned on the two religious channels, Radio Télévision Armée de l'Eternel (RTAE) and Radio Télévision Puissance (RTP) which had made them their speciality.[1]

The Minister had listened to the complaints of the popular theatre troupes who claimed to have been stifled by the rapid success of Nigerian video. It is true that fewer television audiences in Kinshasa were interested in the local theatre productions, filmed on video and televised on the commercial stations. They preferred Nigerian videos which were better conceived and produced, and were packed with special effects.

Broadcast in their original versions, these Nigerian videos had gained much success via the religious channels. Around June 2002 the RTAE station owned by 'General' Sony Kafuta Rockman, and Pastor Kiziamina Kibila's RTP had the idea of using these films in support of evangelism. In order to get the message across, these stations made sure that the films were commented on by bilingual evangelists, who also translated part of the dialogue. Nigerian videos soon broke all audience viewing records.

Two commentators became big stars of the small screen; one of them, nicknamed 'José of Jésus' who was an RTP presenter, made such an impact on his viewers that his house, in the fashionable district of Matonge, was overrun each day by 'fans' desperate to meet him.[2] 'My telephone just did not stop ringing. Sometimes I would get up to a hundred calls after a broadcast,' he recalled.

These viewers, mostly women, told him about their own experiences, asking in the main to be 'cured' of 'mysterious' ailments. One woman that I met at his house claimed to have been cured of infertility thanks to a process for lifting a spell that had been cast on her. (The method had been suggested by the famous television presenter who was known to her through watching Nigerian films).

1. RTAE is a radio-television channel owned by Pastor Sony Kafuta from a church called the Armée de l'Eternel, while the RTP station is owned by Kiziamina Kibila from the revivalist church La Puissance du Nom de Jésus.
2. The presenters Bakajika and José de Jésus gave partial translations of the dialogue as voice-overs. They also commented on the action of certain scenes, citing biblical verses and appealing to the viewers to believe in the power of the word of God. They also called the viewers as witnesses to the events as they unfolded. José de Jésus had in this way made a number of converts. Among the films broadcast like this and given such commentaries were *Suicide Mission* produced by Sunny Collins and Teco Benson, and directed by Fred Amata; *Highway to the Grave* directed by Sonia Cacchus; *Just a Little Sin,* produced and directed by Mike Bamiloye; *The Story of my Life* and *Another Great Mistake* also by Mike Bamiloye; *Timi the Village Girl,* produced by Moses Ebere and Sam Lnisters, and directed by Moses Ebere; and *Dangerous Love.*

**Franck Baku Fuita &
Godefroid Bwiti Lumisa**

Evangelical videos tell all kinds of stories: A married and respectable man is seduced by a young girl who has a siren-like allure and is endowed with magic powers. Spellbound, the man forgets all about his wife. A series of misfortunes befalls him and he loses his job. He can only find peace through prayer and a pastor then releases him from the spell he is under.

Another variant is the married woman who can't have children and goes to see a fetishist/healer who helps her to conceive. The child once born becomes a source of misfortune for the family. Only a pastor can get to the bottom of the mystical force that is causing the family so much grief. During a session of prayer, the child turns into dust, liberating the couple from the grip of the fetishist, who was incarnated in the child sorcerer.

For the actor Elombe Sukari, these Nigerian films are vehicles for fetishist culture and eulogies to sorcery. The supporters of these videos deny the charge; on the contrary, they have been edified by the biblical content of their messages. In fact, even if the majority of Nigerian videos broadcast on Congolese television are dedicated to possession and sorcery, they nearly always have a 'happy ending'. Fetishism and occult forces are always swept away by prayer. For this reason many television viewers find the films edifying: 'They have really helped me re-affirm my Christian beliefs. Thanks to these stories I have rediscovered the path of prayer, which is stronger than fetishism,' explains Annie Mbembaki, a follower of the Ministère du Combat spirituel (Ministry for Spiritual Combat), led by Olangi W'Osho. Nathalie Dimbituno, another disciple of the same church, recalls how evangelical videos changed her life: 'After having watched many Nigerian films, and because of the biblical instruction that I received from them, I left my husband. He wasn't really mine because I was only his second wife.'

In a city like Kinshasa where the chapels of evangelical churches are multiplying, the faithful can be transported just by watching the twice daily doses served up by RTP and RTAE. 'Women drop everything to watch these films. They are seduced by the presenter commentaries which are sometimes very amusing. People feel that they are watching something that relates to their world,' says Nsuala, a video fan. 'Sometimes they are so engaging that even the children spend hours watching them instead of doing their homework,' one teacher confirmed. 'Children's education would have suffered even more if we had kept broadcasting so many of these films.'

Faced with the threat of this 'invasion', actors from Kinshasa carried out a kind of Congolese cultural coup by stopping the transmission of Nigerian films: a great relief to Elombe Sukari, head of the Simba theatre troupe, whose plays (on the private channel Antenne A) had suffered from the competition. The complaints of the Congolese actors put an end to this. Led by Elombe Sukari, secular channels were able to convince the authorities that these films were undermining national production:

> We pay tax in order to broadcast our work, and before that the songs and plays have to be approved by the Board of Censors, but the Nigerian videos are broadcast without the channels paying any tax or paying any royalties to the Nigerian producers.

All the Congolese stations are guilty of unfair competition and act illegally. No royalties are paid for the broadcasting of big feature films which Congolese audiences are desperate to see. The producers of films starring the likes of Arnold Schwarzenegger, Sylvester Stallone, Richard Gere, Bruce Willis, Jean-Claude Van Damme, Jackie Chan and others, also cannot expect anything back from Congolese television. 'Yet many of these films are broadcast and they constitute a large part of the output of these channels,' José de Jésus declares, asking why the authorities have never prevented such piracy on the private commercial channels.

Richard Kazibu, of Kiziamina Kibila's RTP channel believes it was private commercial channels that incited Congolese actors to organize a protest march from the Nigerian Embassy to the Ministry for Culture. The Embassy was coerced into making a verbal memorandum to the Congolese Minister for Press and Information, demanding an end to the broadcasting of such films. The reason given was that the broadcasts were made without the permission of the Nigerian producers; the same reason was given on 12 March 2003 by the Minister for Information when he declared:

> Your channel broadcasts Nigerian films and other programmes which are not regulated by the specifications and declarations of use, especially not by the contracts relating to the use of foreign television programmes.

He ordered them to put their house in order:

> I am reminding you for the last time that the public broadcast of Nigerian films is prohibited according to the diplomatic memorandum that the Nigerian Ambassador sent me in 2001 and which was widely disseminated through the local press. I declare that your channel has taken no notice of this and I ask you to suspend, immediately, the broadcasting of these films, for which you have no authorization for public transmission.

Although it had lost this round, RTP redressed its position by making itself legal, signing a contract on 25 May 2003 with the Andy Best Production company, who were to introduce Nigerian video producers to the Democratic Republic of Congo. But nothing changed. While waiting for the restriction to be lifted, RTP claimed it was ready to 'set fire once more to the small screen'. As for José de Jésus, he did not renounce what he called his 'evangelical work'. He continued to show Nigerian films but only at the prayer meetings where his popularity hadn't abated.

Conscious of strong competition from Nigerian films, Congolese actors didn't restrict themselves to attacks on issues of legality and royalties. They also brought up 'the violent and occultic nature of these celebrated films'. In the words of Elombe Sukari:

> Nigerian films captivate their audiences because they are obscene. Those of us who are more puritanical and have a stronger moral code are unable to imitate this, and this is a limitation. They feed us endless sensational, not to say macabre, scenes full of magic, fetishism and sorcery.

According to him, the viewers who don't know any better, are convinced that the actor Mike who plays the role of the pastor in many Nigerian films, is a pastor in real life, although he is in fact a businessman.[3] One actress called Céline Nzita is more forceful on this:

> We shouldn't be making people believe that these films are religious. In most of the films, God only appears at the end, whereas Satan is there the whole way through. What is the purpose of this, especially when we have always been told that in Nigeria fetishes are on sale in the market just like any other merchandise?

The actors have a difficult job convincing people. Many theatre directors whose work is shown on the Congolese commercial stations claim that they have learnt a great deal from watching Nigerian films, especially about special effects and outside sets.

As to the National Music and Theatre Censor Board, it has never criticized the Nigerian films and does not envisage opposing their return to Congolese television. 'After all,' one of the board members said, 'they are no more violent or obscene than many other big feature films.'

3. Mike Bamiloye who directs and acts in his own films is an authentic evangelist pastor. This does not prevent him from also, and perhaps above all, being a businessman.

Film Profile No. 13
'am in Love
Directed by Andy Chukwu

Date of Release: 2006
Production: OJ International
Filmscript: Chuks Obiora
Camera/Photography:
Mohamed Abullahi
Cast: Chinedu Ikediese & Osita
Iheme

This comedy brings to the screen the midgets Chinedu and Osita, a very popular double-act in Africa,[1] who have inspired many Nigerian producers. Both actors are graduates of Enugu University.

In 'am in Love, Chinedu plays the role of a young pharmacy graduate (Gabriel) who returns to his home village to meet up with his beloved Sandra. This girl is nearly twice his height and her parents think that she is mad to be with him. They oppose her marriage to Gabriel, whom they call the 'small boy'. Things move on for Gabriel/Chinedu when his rival Desmond returns from a prolonged trip to the United States (touting a bandana, gangster shades and a heavy Bronx accent). One day, when he sees Gabriel sitting on Sandra's lap, the 'American' thinks Gabriel is a child and gives him a few coins to go and buy some biscuits.

Desmond soon goes to Sandra's parents to ask for her hand, to the great chagrin of Gabriel who does everything he can to separate them. A friend who is also a midget (Osita Iheme), helps him out. What follows is a series of rather burlesque attempts (including explosions, sabotage and battles of wit) as Chinedu and Osita try to discourage Desmond. Sandra, meanwhile, rebuffs Desmond's advances by pretending that she can't go to live with him in the States and uses a fear of flying as her excuse.

Exasperated, Desmond ends up buying a potent medicine to try to get rid of Gabriel and injects him with it. Gabriel disappears for a few days. When he comes back to the village, he looks to all appearances demented, and is dressed like the archetypal village idiot. Believing that her fiancé has become either a drug-addict or a mad man, Sandra finally agrees to marry Desmond. Gabriel doesn't return to normal until after the wedding, but he decides not to give up and plans his revenge. First of all, he manages to get his accomplice Osita hired as a servant in the couple's house. Then, using his pharmaceutical knowledge, he poisons Desmond's food until he also goes mad.

This is a mediocre film both for its script and its technical quality – yet it is better than the average Nollywood production. It has some

1. In an interview published on www.nigeriamovies.net Chinedu recalls extravagant and indecent behaviour on the part of fans elsewhere on the continent, of a kind not seen in Nigeria.

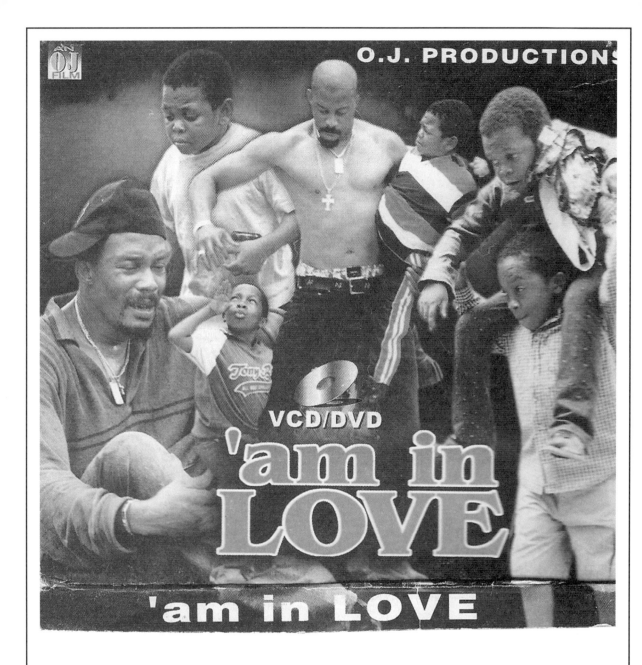

V-CD cover of Andy Chukwu's
'am in Love

good comic moments, despite these being offset by a number of sequences which are scarcely better than rather crude television sketches. *'am in Love* is fairly representative of the series of films featuring the comic duo. A common theme is the lack of inhibition and great tenderness their characters are shown by the tall and striking women they meet, who don't seem to mind at all about them being 'vertically challenged'. The film also revisits, as do many other Nigerian films, the archetype of the 'bad boy' returning from the US, with his pockets full of dollars. Although America holds a certain fascination, it is most often depicted as a sinful place. This leads to some great dialogue, for example when Desmond threatens to 'blow away' Gabriel, whose father responds: 'This is not America, you are not going to shoot anyone'. (Nigeria, of course, being a haven of peace and good-manners when compared to the US). American English is used a great deal in the film, a disconcerting and foreign language in the Nigerian context.

13 Kenya & Nollywood: A State of Dependence
Ogova Ondego

Nigerian videos generate conflicting views in Kenya depending on who one talks to. What is not in doubt, however, is that many Kenyans identify with the stories and themes of Nigerian home-videos which are close to the social realities of their own lives.

The Christian messages put over in these films are particularly appealing to Kenyans, 80 per cent of whom are Christians. The audiences in Kenya seem to be interested only in good stories that are both entertaining and informative, and rarely question the quality of the videos.

According to the actor Bosire Maroro, 'Nigerian videos are well developed in terms of script, character and storyline, unlike Kenyan films that come across as chronicles of events strung together as if they were news recordings.'

'The issue of quality doesn't arise among ordinary people who don't know what constitutes good filmmaking,' says budding filmmaker, Willie Owusu. 'What Kenyans want is a good story on a good theme, that is presented in an entertaining way. If the story appeals, teaches and entertains, then Kenyans don't care about how the film has been put together. Nigerian products are, in any case, better packaged, with nicer pictures on the covers, and better promotional material and posters than the Kenyan equivalents.'

According to Stephen Mukasa a video-distributor, 'Everyone, the churches, the educational institutions, the magicians, or the just plain curious, likes Nigerian home-videos', especially, it seems, for their portrayal of Christianity as more powerful than witchcraft or magic. In his opinion, 'The quality of Nigerian films is high, but the huge demand for them is forcing pirates to duplicate them fast and carelessly, with poor copies that reflect badly on the workmanship of Nigerian filmmakers.'

It is the relevance of their themes – poverty, illness, unemployment, injustice, religion, rituals, culture – that readily connects them with Kenyans who easily identify with these issues. The technical quality may be wanting but these videos are only affordable in Kenya because they are pirated.

Consumers such as Isaac Rop find Nigerian videos 'educative, with more or less no pornographic content, suitable for family viewing because of their Christian messages of hope. We appreciate this quality in the "African context".'

Jane Mbiti, a screenwriter, says ordinary consumers are not film-makers 'bothered with considerations of "themes" and "quality",' as long as the videos 'teach and caution on subjects such as romance, jealousy, wealth, greed and witchcraft.'

'These videos might be cheap, monotonous and not very well produced,' says director Judy Kibinge whose soap *Dangerous Affair* is based on the Nigerian home-video model, 'but at least you get to see African faces on screen.'

Florence Mawanda, who scripts, markets and distributes documentaries for an international non-governmental organization, says she approves of Nigerian films for being 'Afrocentric' and for having 'excellent scripts, gripping and exciting stories, but pirated copying spoils the quality'. In terms of packaging, she remarks that Nigerians 'have got it right: sex, women, witchcraft, anger and bright colors sell!'

Marselina Ouma, a state counsel attached to the newly established Kenya Copyright Board, and senior assistant registrar Bernice Gachegu, agree that Nigerian films are not only 'full of witchcraft' but have 'escapist themes and change your outlook on things'.

Although artist Lydia Gatundu-Galavu finds the films to have 'predictable themes and endings,' she admits that they have 'admirable special effects such as putting a man in a bottle and making people appear and disappear as if they were spirits. The drama is good and has a natural quality.' However, she faults the videos for 'poor sound, and noisy background music that interferes with the dialogue.'

Film director Wanjiru Kinyanjui explains that despite the fact that 'quality may not bother ordinary people as long as they can identify with the characters in the videos ... Nigerian films are of better quality than Kenyan ones: they are simply filmed and provide a form of entertainment that fits with the life experiences of Kenyans.' The simplicity of the filming, she explains, 'enables one to use one's imagination in appreciating the work.'

However, film directors and producers Dommie Yambo-Odotte and Jane Murago-Munene do not find these films to be 'anything Kenyans can be proud of or learn anything from', as they are 'poorly produced on budgets that are so low that it is degrading.'

Harrison Kamau, a law student, feels that it doesn't matter which language Nigerians use in their films as 'the dialogue is spoken with a heavy accent, so you don't know whether they are speaking vernacular, Pidgin or English.'

Nigerians also punctuate their videos with proverbs and sayings in vernacular, usually without translations or subtitles. This, Jane Mbiti argues, is an indication that the primary audience is not international but mainly Nigerian, able to understand the message in its context. Nigerian characters may speak an English that is difficult for some but it hasn't prevented Kenyans from translating the videos into languages such as Kiswahili and Kikuyu, when they are screened in video-clubs and other makeshift theatres. Here, commentators explain what is going on to viewers as the action progresses.

The actor Bukeko particularly enjoys videos in Pidgin English which he finds very comical. A good film, according to film director Brutus Sirucha, should be understood irrespective of the language in which it is made.

Nigerian videos are thought to have made an impact in Kenya at various levels. Some people think the theme of witchcraft draws Kenyans into 'backwardness' and 'immorality'. The scriptwriter Jane Mbiti identifies

> a heightened interest in witchcraft. Hitherto well-educated, progressive Christians no longer frown on notions of consulting witch-doctors, mediums, or medicine men as was the case before the appearance of Nigerian videos in Kenya. People now admit they are consulting spirit-mediums about problems they consider beyond human control.

She points out that 'Some churches in Nairobi have gone on the offensive, preaching against Nigerian videos and labelling them "immoral".'

Judy Kibinge, producer of *Dangerous Affair*, argues that Nigerian videos present a stereotypical view of West Africans and leave Kenyans wondering whether their sole preoccupations are love, witchcraft and money. According to the image portrayed in the films, Nigerians are controlled either by witchcraft or religion. They also portray the Nigerian male as being controlled by his wives and mistresses, who use charms and magic to try to strip him of his property.

But Nigerian films do have some positive effects. For example, they are filling the gap left by the virtual standstill in Kenyan film production. The Kenyan government has issued a guideline to local television stations to ensure that 20 per cent of their broadcasts are locally made.

Kenyans are also taking inspiration from Nigerian styles of clothing. Notable examples of this are politicians Peter Anyang Nyong'o, Paul Gor Sunguh, Koigi wa Wamwere and Raila Amolo Odinga who even appear in Parliament in Nigerian *agbadas*. Other Kenyans are adopting the names of popular characters from Nigerian films, such as 'Awilo Sharp Sharp' and 'Aki na Ukwa'.

Nigerian video-films have helped to cultivate a sense of African pride, popularizing African styles of dressing, and affirming certain local aesthetic values, such as the taste for larger women. Some commentators add that Nigerian films are educating Kenyans not only about such things as special effects in filmmaking, but about social life, and about ways of dealing with witchcraft and hypocrisy in society. In this way a dialogue is taking place between Nigeria and Kenya. Moreover, Nigerian films show the similarities across African societies in gender relations, power hierarchies and other social relationships – a good starting point for socio-cultural interaction.

It is also said that Nigerian films are encouraging Kenyans to view the medium of video positively and not necessarily as something that is inferior to celluloid as previously. Not only have they helped Kenyans to understand that there is an alternative to Hollywood, but they have also introduced them to a formula for making low-budget films.

As many videos highlight social conflict, they enable Kenyans to evaluate their own lifestyle in relation to modern and traditional ways. Most of the films produced in Kenya have been commissioned and financed by institutions with the aim of making issue-based films for raising social awareness. Nigerian films, on the other hand, are usually financed by individuals and made purely for entertainment. Consequently, they introduce Kenyans to the idea that films can be made not just for enlightening people about issues such as domestic violence, girls' education or female circumcision,[1] but also for the equally valid goal of 'spectacle' itself.

1. In fact, these themes are addressed in a number of Nigerian videos but they are not at all didactic in style. Their main objective is to tell a story, while many of the awareness-raising films subsidized all over Africa by local public offices, NGOs, or international organizations have in mind above all the message that they want to put across, and only make use of fiction if it supports this aim. It is likely that the Nigerian approach has a greater impact. Films such as *The Mourning After, Late Marriage* or *Widow* (on the situation of widows in society), *The Colours of Tomorrow* and *The Apple* (on young marriage and the risk of vaginal fistulas) are certainly more effective than any kind of awareness-raising production tackling the same themes.

V-CD cover of
Francis Onwochei's
Claws of the Lion

Film Profile No. 14
Claws of the Lion
Directed by Francis Onwochei

Sheila is alone in her apartment in Lagos which she shares with three other students. She is crying in front of the magnificent cake that she has made for her birthday. Her cad of a fiancé has forgotten to turn up. Her less naïve student-flatmates find her in tears and take advantage of her by making her go with them to a celebration organized by a western ambassador. He is fond of seducing 'young flesh', paying his entourage handsomely in dollars for their efforts to find him gorgeous girls. Kachi, friend and tout for this libidinous ambassador, is a former Nigerian army captain who served during the war in Sierra Leone. A flash-back shows Kachi injecting himself with heroin before raping a young Sierra Leonean girl taken captive by his men.

When Sheila realizes she has fallen into a trap, she asks if she can make a phone call but Kachi manages to buy some time and persuade her that she is not a prisoner. Torn between fear and desire for revenge against her unpardonable fiancé, Sheila ends up falling for the charms of Kachi. He wins her over with a tale about his retraining as a sharp-shooter; he claims he works for a vet involved in zoos and the protection of wildlife. She is so won over that she confides in him that she has never known her father: he had abandoned her mother when she refused to have an abortion. Kachi pretends to be tender and protective and leads her gently to his bedroom. When Sheila discovers that Kachi is in fact a violent addict, it is too late. She tries to escape but he floors her with the dart gun he uses to put wild animals to sleep. Raped by Kachi, then by his friends, Sheila is taken back home, barely able to walk and in a state of shock.

A victim of misfortune, she is hospitalized for the first time. Her fiancé is panic-stricken, but she cannot forgive him. As for the students who put her in Kachi's clutches: they believe they have redeemed themselves by bringing her a haul of dollars. Sheila rejects them with all the contempt she can muster in her weak state. Three months later, she has a fainting fit and is hospitalized once more in a serious condition. Her mother and her step-father run to her bedside and find out, one, that she is pregnant and two, that she

Date of release: 2006
Production: Frankochei Productions
Filmscript: Tosin James Atega & Remi Pereira
Cast: Keppy Bassey Ekpeyong, Ekwi Onwuemene, Empress Njamah, Ashley Nwosu, Francis Onwochei & Laurent Vanderelst

Film Profile No. 14
Claws of the Lion

is HIV-positive. At the same time, a slightly anxious Kachi turns up at the hospital for news of Sheila. He meets a doctor who had made him have an HIV test some months earlier. Through a flash-back we learn that the captain left the army after a first HIV-positive test which he never took seriously. Inside the confines of the hospital, Kachi finds out that he is responsible for Sheila's pregnancy and for her contamination. On top of that, Sheila's mother was none other than the fiancé that he had abandoned twenty years earlier and finally that Sheila is thus his own daughter. Ex-Captain Kachi runs home, locks the door and holds a pistol to his head, while an unremitting sequence of his predatory acts, all of which have led him to this end, is played out in his head.

This film, with its stifling story, was screened for the first time during the Lagos Film Forum in July 2005. The Zimbabwean film producer Ben Zulu, also head of the African Film Development Fund, was in the cinema. With his professional antennae alert, he wasn't totally convinced by the hour and a half version shown that day but he immediately detected in the film a diamond in the rough that just needed to be shaped. With the producer's agreement, he took on the task of pruning *Claws of the Lion*, cutting all its overlong and awkward sections and some of its unwieldy sequences. Cut to 45 minutes, it became incomparably better and was honoured at three successive film festivals in Nigeria: the Abuja Festival, the Festival of the International Conference on AIDS and Sexually Transmitted Infections in Africa in 2005, and the Zuma Film Festival in 2006, before being shown at several international gatherings. Particularly noted was the very convincing performance by first-time actress, Ekwi Onwuemene in the role of Sheila.

14 Is the Nigerian Model Fit for Export?[1]
Olivier Barlet

▶▶

Is the development of home-video in Nigeria a model for the rest of Africa? Should certain elements be adopted, and are there any lessons to be learned?

Development in a specific context directly related to the economic & political environment

The end of the oil boom, the deterioration of the balance of trade, and the dollar's increase in value vis-à-vis the weak Naira sealed the fate of Nigerian cinema. Celluloid film production costs became prohibitive. Many filmmakers left the country to try to work in London or New York because of the military dictatorship. Finally, the rise in crime and corruption made the streets of the major towns so unsafe at night that people preferred to stay at home. The terrain was ripe for home-video to emerge as the ideal, risk-free source of entertainment. In the meantime, film theatres started to close down or were taken over by the churches that flourish in such moments of crisis and disorientation.

In this context, and given that the satellite channels, and particularly the South African channels, were flooded by American action films, three types of productions emerged to meet public demand:

- films that evoke local cultural roots by updating legends;
- films that play on urban fears with stories about, for example, vigilantes;
- films that explore social or emotional issues in an endogenous style.

A profitable but dwindling activity

When Mr Holy Rock wondered how best to put to profit a cargo of blank video tapes that arrived at the Lagos docks from Taiwan at the end of the eighties, he heard about the profits people were making selling pre-recorded video tapes in Ghana (the first video production *Zinoba* was a big commercial hit in 1987). As there was nothing worth using on television, he had the first Yoruba-language story shot on VHS. It was an immediate hit and was instantly copied. *Living in Bondage*, made by Chris Obi Rapu (under the pseudonym 'Vic Mordi')

1. The notes that form this chapter were written in 2002 for the French Ministry of Foreign Affairs as part of an evaluation of French cooperative politics in the domain of film.

Retailer promotes the latest releases of V-CDs in Ikoyi, Lagos, 2007
(© Robert Minangoy)

in 1992, an Ibo-language story of a man who signs a pact with the devil to get rich, was a huge hit. *Living in Bondage II* followed just a few months later. By 1994, production had taken off and the Idumota district of Lagos's central market became devoted to home-video.

Making a killing was, and remains, the main motivation behind these productions. Video production, which today supplies 15,000 video clubs around the country (only 4,000 are registered, paying a tax of US$ 58), and individual cassette sales, which can reach up to 200,000 copies of the same film, are the result of a logic by which people try to appeal simply in order to sell. Production is financed by the people who distribute the films, who are known as 'marketers' and who function without any other backing than the revenues they generate.

In the course of the first half of 2002, the marketers, who had noted a fall in sales, agreed not to produce any films for three months (from March to May 2002) in order to sell off their existing stocks ('to rehabilitate the sector'). The saturation of the market also came at a time when the profession, which had developed empirically without any kind of formal organization, was seeking a second wind and was worried about the competition that would inevitably force the country's markets to open up. The huge rise in the number of producers (260 in 2001) and productions (two a day on average, one a week in Ghana) made it harder to make a film profitable. This in turn led to a fall in production budgets (from US$ 6,500 to US$ 50,000, and US$ 13,000 on average) and thus a drop in quality, which was already substandard.

Interest has indeed flagged. Productions have grown so repetitive (always the same tired old recipes) that the public is now bored, under the impression that they are always seeing the same old thing. This confirms an old film saying: no profits, no cinema; but no creativity, no cinema either.

Video has never reached the same stature as cinema

That is not to say that there are no real artists. Filmmakers suffer from not being able to shoot real celluloid films, or to make films with budgets that guarantee even a minimum level of quality.

Contrary to what might have been hoped, the filmmakers trained in Western film schools (Saddik Balewa, Newton Aduaka, Odion P. Agboh, etc.) have not entered the home-video circuits, trying instead to make films with foreign funding (French Ministry of Foreign Affairs, M-Net New Directions, etc.). Odion P. Agboh's *Twins of the Rainforest*, funded by M-Net and one of the best recent productions, has been screened in many foreign festivals, but has not been seen in Nigeria. Amaka Igwe has also made a film in similar conditions, but it is hard to distribute abroad because its Nigerian English is difficult to understand.

Nigerian films were much awaited at the 2001 Fespaco (notably two shot on film by Ladi Ladebo), but proved to be a disappointment, revealing all the failings of home-video (screenplays based entirely on the dialogues, highly theatrical acting styles, dull camera work and effects, poor sound tracks, etc.).

There is thus a clear divide between the two sectors, one of which continues to flourish, even if it is in crisis, the other of which is practically non-existent and invisible, but which is crying out to exist.

The desire for cinema is still strong

There is no denying the dynamism of the market or audience interest in endogenous images. Every Sunday afternoon, Lagos's Yoruba population heads off en masse to the National Theatre where Yoruba videos ('Juju videos', from the word for 'magic' in Yoruba) are shown from midday to 9 pm. There are screenings every three hours, and everyone meets up afterwards in the neighbourhood bars (*abegi*). Spectators often buy videos of the films they see at the National Theatre so that they can watch them again at home. This shows that people still enjoy going out to the films (that is, going to see a film in a movie theatre with friends or family), a desire that can potentially be capitalized on once security improves.

The South African company Nu Metro has understood this, and plans to build eight multiplex theatres in various Nigerian towns. The danger facing Nigerian production will then be that the American 35mm productions distributed by Nu Metro throughout English-speaking Africa's 226 screens will take over as they have everywhere else.

Several key figures stand out in this climate of self-sufficiency
Given the foreign competition, Nigerian productions will not be saved by endlessly churning out the same old recipes, however successful they have been. Salvation no doubt lies in improving the quality of the way in which themes are treated, themes that are developed to meet public expectations.

In this production context, very many young people desperately want to get into film. The terrain is ripe for young artists to emerge, but they do so with no training, through capillary action, depending on connections with the financial backers.

A handful of director-producers who care about the artistic quality of their films, have taken an original path in this respect, notably Tunde Kelani, Zeb Ejiro, Femi Lasode, Amaka Igwe, and Mahmood Ali-Balogun. Faced with the power of the marketers, they have developed their own production and distribution networks. Tunde Kelani was trained as a film cameraman in television long before video was developed. He filmed newsreel, documentaries, sports, drama inserts, and so on, for use on television. Every television station had a film laboratory and processed and edited its film material in-house. Kelani was a student at the London Film School where he did a diploma course in the Art and Technique of filmmaking, and returned to Nigeria by which time video had been introduced for news coverage. He photographed no less than twenty feature films before he started directing. By this time, Nigeria's economy had collapsed and it was no longer possible to fund films. He started out by using video in another way, as a story teller, and was looking for an appropriate technology in which to film stories. He therefore gained a lot of experience in digital filmmaking and introduced the mobile cinema using digital projector and sound equipment to take the cinema to the people. He owns an impressive plant that reproduces V-CDs with shelf-loads of duplicating machines.

The promo methods developed by Zeb Ejiro in particular, who studied marketing in Britain, have proved to be highly effective. A video release is treated like a real event. Previews are organized, where wealthy Nigerians pay a very high price (US$ 20 to US$ 40) to be seen (which sometimes already recoups a considerable part of the film's cost); rows of posters are billed without any authorization in the street; trailers of the films are shown on video and television; promo campaigns featuring the film stars are organized on radio and television; coverage is organized in the three specialist showbiz actor and film magazines (*Fame, National Encomium,* and *City People*). Distribution works very efficiently through a network of a multitude of retail outlets (hawkers, street stalls, market stalls, hairdressers and other shops, etc.) before it is even possible for the pirates to get themselves organized. The international distribution works via websites that distribute cassettes to Nigerian communities abroad.

These directors, however, stand out above all for their cinematic approach. They combine a desire to raise public awareness of a variety of social issues (prostitution, Aids, corruption, urban violence, etc.) and the desire not to alienate their audiences, hence the inclusion of action scenes, special effects, and stars. They class their films somewhere between auteur and popular film. Working independently of the marketers, they control their own film content and the duration of the shoots. Whereas most films are shot in under a week and then very quickly completed, Tunde Kelani spends about 20 days shooting, between eight to ten weeks editing, and four weeks on the soundtrack.

The video sector represents a real economic force
With average sales since the crisis[2] of 10,000 to 12,000 copies per film (compared to 60,000 to 70,000 at the start of the home-video boom) and a declared production of nearly 700 films, Nigerian home-video turnover appears, despite the lack of reliable figures, to represent over US$ 80 million dollars according to the National Film and Video Censors Board (NFVCB). The sector is thought to have created nearly 3,000 to 4,000 jobs in the space of ten years. Home-video exports represent a turnover of over US$ 950,000. Hausa films produced in Kano are very popular in travelling video-clubs in Niger, as are Yoruba films in Benin and Togo. Cassettes dubbed into French are sold in various French-speaking African countries, and cassettes in English have invaded markets in neighbouring countries and as far afield as Zambia and South Africa. Distribution on the Internet has opened up access to the diaspora.

The Nigerian home-video model is not exportable
The Nigerian home-video boom has its roots in a very specific local context, notably: high insecurity levels that forced people to stay at home in the evenings; the collapse of the Naira vis-à-vis the dollar, making production costs prohibitive; local businessmen's pragmatism; a strong local culture and the importance of the ethnic factor (Yoruba theatre, urban Igbo themes, local languages); a traditional Nigerian

2. The moratorium on new release films that was declared in 2002 had one advantage in allowing production to regenerate itself and output has doubled since that time.

cinema that already paved the way; the sharp rise in the number of VCRs and V-CD players in homes.

Home-video has developed almost completely free of any regulations or organization of the profession. It's a case of the survival of the fittest. Exploitation and many other kinds of scams are widespread (for example, underpaid professionals, recycling of unsold cassettes causing images to jump and colours to fade).

Nigerian home-video has developed on the back of existing markets. Cheaply made Nigerian productions have invaded markets in neighbouring countries (Ghana, Cameroon, Niger, Benin, and the African market in general) thanks to dumping and aggressive sales practices. Pirating (of Ghanaian productions, for example) is rife. A unique model of cinematic production has thus emerged which risks undermining cinema for a long time. The mercantile sex and violence contained in the Nigerian videos that are exported and broadcast without carrying any warnings, undermine the cultural values of the countries concerned (Ghana has thus been swamped by videos that are an affront to local moral values, whereas its own video productions respect them).

The need to produce at a low cost deprecates the artists who are forced to associate their names with mediocre products to survive.

The films only recoup their costs if copies sell well. As sales have slowed down, investors are showing less interest and are starting to lose faith in the sector, looking for other fields in which to make profits. Such are the shortcomings of a system based solely on business and which so cruelly lacks structure and regulation.

The Nigerian model offers some undeniable assets

Video is part of a film's commercial lifespan (in the following order: theatre release, video release, broadcast on fee-paying television, on public television, on planes and in hotels). In South Africa, video distribution doubles or triples a film's revenues. Video's success in Nigeria suggests that there is the potential to distribute film products profitably.

There is a great deal to be learnt from the promo methods developed by the Nigerians, including their poster campaigns, trailers, specialist magazine coverage, radio and television coverage. The same goes for their original selling methods which are truly in touch with their audiences, notably the many street stalls, hawkers, sales in hairdressers, the multiplication of video-clubs, promo events such as those in Ghana where floats go round, their teams offering cassettes to passer-bys). Sponsoring by car firms, drinks companies and hotels. is also very common.

Nigerian productions offer a popular film form that is close to the audience's preoccupations and reflects their daily lives (comedies of manners), fears (urban violence), legends (Yoruba myths), and the supernatural realm (witchcraft).

The organized star system means that the actors are a real promotional asset for the films. This is fuelled by purely sensationalist media coverage that may well be superficial (often focusing on their private lives), but which is also effective.

Nigerian professionals unanimously insist on the sense of pride the success of the sector gives them. They see the phenomenon as proof that Africa has the potential to produce its own images without foreign backing. They would like to represent Nigeria at international film festivals and are conscious that this can help them to improve Nigeria's image around the world.

Home-video professionals are anxious to make the most of the advantages of digital technology on shoots and in broadcasting to improve quality (DVD players are affordable in Nigeria, costing around US$ 58). Efforts to develop new markets have encouraged people to experiment with film dubbing in order to be able to distribute further afield. Dubbing is hindered, however, by the lack of an international version at the shooting stage, which makes it impossible to dub the original sound track.

Having a social message opens up additional distribution circuits, such as public screenings in universities, travelling film buses (Zeb Ejiro's *Domitilla*, a film about prostitution, was such a hit that the term is now commonly used to refer to prostitutes; Kelani screened the Zimbabwean film *Yellow Card* in 200 schools, even reaching Benin, thanks to a regional grant).

The professional milieu is beginning to organize itself, especially the actors (the National Association of Nigerian Theatre Arts Practitioners (NANTAP) and the Nigerian Actors' Guild (NAG). Marketers are also becoming more organized (more concentrated around several dynamic companies, such as Infinity and Kas-video), and together agreed on a voluntary production recess. Trade seminars have been held, such as the Onitsha seminar in June 2002, where basic rules were adopted to supervise the recovery of video-club takings, and to negotiate with the Video Club Owners Association of Nigeria (VCOAN). The sector's dynamism has enabled centripetal forces to emerge, notably bodies that are looking for quality, such as the Committee for Relevant Arts, which edits the *City Art Guide*, a free cultural magazine, and organizes a Cinema Carnival in Lagos every September. Media influence, which gives widespread coverage to new video releases, is growing, thereby enabling film critics to emerge. Dailies such as *The Guardian* or *The Comet* publish long articles on the sector and its new productions. As the sector becomes more organized, it is able to offer local answers to the advertisers' and NGO's commissions. Following the American model, sequels of hit films are shot, such as *Issakaba* 1, 2, 3 and 4.

Intense video production is formative. Instead of waiting for a hypothetical shoot to happen, people get out there and make films. If professionals were given access to the training programmes they ask for, they could considerably improve the quality of their productions. The sector's development has facilitated the democratization of image production and the emergence of young filmmakers and film technicians.

A wide range of needs

The propensity for imitation means that it is possible to imagine that an improvement in the quality of certain films would benefit the entire sector.

It is thus vital to meet the very clear need for training, which is lacking at all levels, from technical aspects to directing.

As production budgets are too small to guarantee a minimum standard of production, it is important to increase budgets, which presupposes new sales strategies if no other form of backing is made available. Using dubbing and sub-titles as a means to break into an African distribution circuit, and gaining access to African and satellite television could give the necessary boost.

One need frequently expressed by the evaluation team's interlocutors is for the sector to open up to the outside, as the country has remained isolated for a long time over its 20 years of military rule. The two forums organized by ITPAN in 2001 and 2002 in collaboration with the French Embassy and the Nigerian Film Corporation (NFC) were thus greatly appreciated because they attracted outside participants. Co-productions seem to them to be the best way of opening up film funding and improving quality. Contacts with producers are particularly sought after in this context. The professionals care about Nigeria's image abroad and would like to be more present on the international film scene, especially at festivals. They would also like greater visibility on the Internet.

International backing has become an objective, but still remains hazy and inaccessible. The general impression is that you have to do a lot of paperwork with very little hope of a favourable outcome. This suggests that there is a need for some kind of technical assistance in compiling and correcting proposals especially to overcome translation problems. When a bad translation was presented before a commission of the French Ministry of Foreign Affairs, via the French Embassy, of *Amazons of Afrika* by Obafemi B. Lasode (who also directed *Shango*, one of the most accomplished Yoruba films), it meant that he stood no chance of getting a positive response. Yet no explanation was given for the refusal.

The majority of the people cited by the evaluation team spoke of investment in better digital equipment as the prerequisite for developing and improving film quality. Sound remains these films' greatest weakness. People recognize and explicitly state the general need to improve sound techniques (both poor sound recording on shoots and back-street cassette duplication being to blame for the low standards).

From celluloid to digital
Although there is a desire to return to shooting on celluloid again – *Amazons of Afrika*'s 30 million Naira budget (US$ 300,000) will enable the director to shoot on celluloid film and *Shango* was shot on both film and video, even though the 15 million Naira budget was insufficient to complete the film version – for practical reasons the future will clearly be digital (closure of cinemas, lack of equipment and means, zero public backing). Digital indeed offers a way of combining both film and video approaches.

Digital screenings are a possibility for the future, especially as there is already a perceptible tendency to re-open cinemas as security gradually improves. Nu Metro is building a chain of multiplexes in Nigeria, but these will be used to screen Hollywood, and occasionally South African, productions.

The difficulties posed by pirating still need to be resolved
Video pirating is rampant. The Ghanaian director Socrate Safo has described how the Nigerians even go as far as changing the credits and adding scenes with their own actors in order to give the films greater commercial appeal when they pirate Ghanaian films!

It is the very people who sell videos who are responsible for the pirating. They do not respect the contracts and print their own cassette covers for the films they distribute, instead of using the covers supplied by the producers, which serve as a basis for calculating the royalties owed. Pirating is also rampant in the video stalls, but the marketers sometimes carry out harsh punitive raids on the guilty parties.

Despite the importance of the Nigerian television network (70 regional channels), television does not yet represent a way of financing films. Films are either pirated (unauthorized programmes with no broadcasting contracts), or traded for advertising space for the next production (three minute spots for a feature film). There are hardly any documentaries. Yet there is great potential. The Nigerian answer to pirating is above all to bulk release a film on all circuits at the same time in order to beat the pirates to it.

Epilogue

Pierre Barrot

If the saying that 'happy people do not have any history' is true, then Nigerians must be unfortunate indeed to have produced the many depressing stories that feed the home-video industry. For every farce, such as the refreshing *Osuofia in London*, or every Hausa musical comedy, there are a thousand morbid melodramas, gory epics and terrifying films about witchcraft.

Despite the desperate content of many Nigerian films,[1] they also have an astonishing vitality. There is more than enough despair but never total hopeless depression. Onookome Okome, cited in the Nigerian revue *Glendora*, describes home-video as an antidote to the moral misery of African cities:

> Home-videos are gradually and effectively replacing all contending forms of popular discourse in many African cities. It seems the era of cheap literatures is gone, replaced by cheap indigenous video productions. These video dramas now form one of the most significant ways in which the city discusses itself, its superficial modernity and its strange attachment to traditional life. In many ways, these dramas construct the city in its own image, sometimes reducing the problem of the city to the pleasure of gazing, the need to feed one's voyeuristic curiosity, but they provide a new and refreshing way to look at the city. This is a medium of the city, created and nurtured in the city for its own benefit. Home video production is itself a direct result of a declining standard in the culture and economics of African city life. It is in a sense a movement out of the purely literary culture. It is a means of discussing tradition and modernity in the city. It is a means through which city dwellers in Africa try to make sense of wretched lives; in other words, it is a means through which city dwellers convince themselves that life is still worth living.[2]

Home-video might be replacing popular literature, but there are definite similarities in their modes of expression. In Africa there was never a huge output equivalent to 'pulp fiction', mainly due to lower levels of literacy and the lack of a disposable income, but popular

1. Violence and suicide are commonplace in these films to an extent that is rarely seen elsewhere.

2. See the article 'Loud in Lagos: Home Video', *Glendora Review*, African Quarterly on the Arts, vol. 2, no. 1, 1997: 75–83.

fiction of this kind does exist in some places and in Francophone Africa it hasn't yet been displaced by home-video. In Abidjan, Isaie Biton Coulibaly had great success with his short stories published in the review *Amina*, and gathered in anthologies such as *Ah les femmes! Ah les hommes!* In Ouagadougou, Noraogo Sawadogo has a loyal audience for his *Nouvelles du vendredi* published in the daily paper *Le Pays*. [3]

In neither case, even with stories less sordid than those coming out of Nigeria, do they give a very optimistic view of society and human nature. Deception, jealousy, fraud and betrayal are the main ingredients.

However, the *Adoras* collection launched in Abidjan a few years ago, has taken a different approach: by firing the imagination with stories shamelessly steeped in sentimentality this collection has broken all sales records. One of the stories was adapted for the cinema by Franco-Ivoirienne producer Martine Ducoulombier under the title *Le pari de l'amour*:[4] a young and beautiful apprentice hairdresser wins on the lottery and makes her dream to become a model in Paris come true. Of course, she is tricked by a sham impresario. But all's well that ends well and she returns to Abidjan (with some of her wealth remaining) and marries someone from home, who she had loved all along but had stupidly jilted when fame and fortune had gone to her head.

Which of these is of more value: the over-played sentimentality of the soaps or the morbid naturalism of the gutter? This debate is part of the long controversy over 'Afro-pessimism' and the 'image of Africa'. Some journalists and writers maintain that western media portray the African continent in a very negative way and that it is essential to correct this. Many people are engaged in this task. International organizations and NGOs, through their press offices, broadcast 'success stories' whose purpose is to show an 'Africa that is winning': these are a string of edifying stories, many of which are no more representative of the reality than the scourges portrayed by the international media (Aids, corruption, civil war and famine).

Antoine Labey, freelance journalist and news writer for Radio Africa No. 1, puts it succinctly: 'There is no positive news or negative news. There is only true news or false news.'

Very often, when western (but also African) media are anxious to give 'positive' information, they produce misinformation. Development gurus and 'do-gooders' set themselves the task of straightening out a continent, but their words only exist in a discourse of propaganda and in the well-intentioned illusions of publicists preoccupied with the question of the 'image of Africa'.

There are two advantages to the dark world of Nigerian videos: the image they portray is neither dictated nor controlled by outsiders or by government. This by no means guarantees that what is shown is 100 per cent truthful, but such videos have a chance of being closer to the

3. Both writers have seen their work adapted for the screen, the first in a mini-series called *Ah, les femmes!*, the second by writing scripts for the *Taxi Brousse* series

4. This film (directed by Didier Aufort) was shot on video, then copied onto film and released in cinemas on 35mm. It was dubbed in English in 2006 with Ghanaian actors.

Pierre Barrot

truth. And if they are depressing, then this is because life can also be depressing. If you want to change the world, claims the iconic French reporter Albert Londres[5] 'you need to apply a pen to the wound'. This is what the scriptwriters of Nigerian films are doing every day.[6]

Many critics from outside, even if they allow the social use of Nigerian videos, still despair about the technical mediocrity and the refusal of most to be artistically ambitious. Many even see the domination of home-video as an obstacle to the rebirth of Nigerian cinema. This fear is not completely unfounded as the obsession with a quick profit (the 'take the money and run' philosophy) is so prevalent that in most cases it prevents an artistic approach. A work of art is characterized by its universal and immortal appeal, whereas 'Nollywood' is characterized by the opposite, by a sense of the particular and the immediate. Yet Nigerian video, in its productive frenzy, is impressive for its inventiveness, for the emotional strength of it actors and for the dramatic intensity of its stories.[7] There is talent enough for a cinematic tradition to emerge from this, and it is expected. There was some scepticism in 2004 when Jeta Amata, a typical Nollywood director, turned to shooting on film, especially when he took for his first attempt an historic subject inspired by the epic story of John Newton, the English slave-trader operating from the Calabar coast at the end of the eighteenth century. A costume drama with slave ships, muskets, swords and telescopes, was quite a challenge in a country where nothing had been shot on 35mm since 1992. But Jeta Amata, a young man of barely 30 years of age, had already made 30 video films, and had no doubt about his ability to carry it off. His audacity, resourcefulness and his energy, as well as abundant self-confidence, worked wonders: people were seduced by his ambition and he managed to get the support of the governor Donald Duke, of British producer Alicia Arce and of actor Nick Moran, whom he knew from making another BBC documentary. *Amazing Grace*, was shot in 2004, with a technical crew and several actors coming from England, and was edited the following year in Los Angeles. The film was completed, in May 2006, two days before it was screened at the Cannes Film Festival. The audience was struck by its high production standards (when compared to the poor technical quality of many African films), and by the achievement of it being put together so well with what was regarded as a derisorily low budget, and by European standards, an astonishing one. But people's reaction to the plot and its execution was more reserved: stereotypical characterization, acting that was over-theatrical, inconsistent historical context, (with modern evangelical clichés super-imposed in an unconvincing way over the brutal reality of the conditions of the slave ships, and the redemption of Newton, the slave-trader, being pure fantasy).[8] Jeta Amata had perhaps taken on too great a challenge when he left more familiar

5. Albert Londres' pen was able to bring about the closure of Cayenne prison. (This prison in French Guyana was the inspiration behind the novel and film *Papillon* starring Steve McQueen.) The reporter was so shocked by what he saw that he pursued it further, taking the campaign as far as Parliament itself. While he was reporting on the story, a prisoner taught him something about journalism: 'It's not for us to say, its for you to see' [ce n'est pas à nous de dire, c'est à vous de voir]'. Albert Londres gave his name to the equivalent prize in France to the Pulitzer.

6. It is striking that many Nollywood scriptwriters used to be journalists, for example, Tosin James Atega, scriptwriter for *Claws of the Lion.* One of his latest scripts for *Children of the Full Moon* (not yet filmed at the time of writing) really captures the practices of certain Nigerian politicians (corruption, political assassination, human sacrifice) by drawing on actual events.

7. Notable among Nigerian filmmakers are Niji Akanni, Amos Oyiwe, Chikeh Ibekwe, Femi Kayode, Tosin James Atega, not forgetting Tunde Babalola (who lives in Britain).

8. This seems to be a characteristic of 'epic' Nigerian films. The verisimilitude which makes the contemporary home-video so effective, is often abandoned in favour of an exaggerated production, and a style of acting which is pantomime-like, bordering on the grotesque (see, for example, *Sango*, *Oduduwa* and, the more recent *Sitanda*).

132

territory to throw himself into a storyline which required a much better grasp of the historical context

But does any of this matter? The film was made. It was then distributed by the South African company Nu Metro. The floodgates are now open and it is possible for other Nigerian producers to be swept along with this tide. When in 2007, Newton Aduaka, was awarded first prize at the Ouagadougou Pan-African Film Festival for *Ezra*, the Nollywood heavyweights were elated by his success, even though it had very little to do with Nigeria itself. Coming to Lagos five years previously for the Film Forum, Aduaka (having previously been resident in London), was given mild acclaim by the doyens of home-video, as it was felt he was cut off from the realities of the market and the public, irreversibly westernized, and thus lost to Nigeria. Yet, *Ezra*, having won an award, was embraced by national pride, even though the film was produced in France, inspired by the civil war in Sierra Leone and filmed in Rwanda.

In Nollywood, two forces run in parallel: that of pride and that of the competitive spirit. Many producers ask the question 'If he can do it, then why can't I?' With their combination of audacity and ingenuousness, it would not be surprising if Nigerian producers turned once again to cinema. Funding is the key issue. There is money in this oil-producing state, but it has never really been invested in filmmaking. Financially, Nollywood is a closed circuit: its income is reinvested in production; bank loans are rare, as is patronage of any kind. In this regard, Jeta Amata was innovative in securing money from a governor, from oil companies and banks, extracting a guaranteed minimum income from a distributor, and even in securing foreign investment.[9]

There is no doubt that certain producers are capable of raising the kind of budgets that cinema require (Kingsley Ogoro was a pioneer in the making of his big-budget film *Across the Niger* which was distributed through the cinema network). But are those who get the financial backing actually those with the most artistic talent for filmmaking? The real artists (Tunde Kelani, Tade Ogidan, Jimi Odumosu and a handful of others) are, according to themselves, the least successful in the Nigerian system at getting funding. Is this a case of 'The man with a head is looking for a cap and the man with the cap lacks a head'.[10]

This equation is even more difficult to resolve when a certain national pride makes co-productions with partners from other countries less likely. Moreover, foreign producers who are open to investing in Nigeria are worried by the poor security situation and by the many risks in a country which, by international standards, is considered chaotic, and whose professionals have a reputation of being untrustworthy. On top of this, the regulations imposed by the National Film Corporation on films shot with foreign crews are such that the incentives to come to Nigeria would have to be very great to

9. French support for production through Fonds Image Afrique and help with distribution from the Africa Cinemas programme funded by the European Union and Agence de la Francophonie.
10. Citing Wole Soyinka's *The Road*, in *Collected Plays, One*, Oxford University Press, 1996,

offset people's reservations about working in the country.

Co-production is discussed at length at each Lagos Film Forum but the conditions for its development are far from being realized. Every year, Michael Auret, head of the Cape Town World Cinema Festival and the Sithengi Film and TV Market, comes to Nigeria looking for potential partners and films to export. During one of his visits he implied that Nollywood was hopeless. In his opinion, even an exceptional film like *Dangerous Twins* is unmarketable, unfit for international distribution because of its technical faults (the near-absence of mixing) and its contempt for established norms (the over-indulgent length and the use of pirated music). According to him, Nollywood's potential will never be realized outside of its own informal networks, except through 're-makes'. This means that filmmakers from outside will re-work the Nigerian stories and turn them into films that will be accepted internationally. The only example to date of this for a Nollywood film is the re-editing of Francis Onwochei's film *Claws of the Lion* by Zimbabwean director Ben Zulu. The latter was planning to produce another full-length Nigerian film (*The Seven Crossroads*) but he had to postpone it due to an unresolved disagreement with the director. The South African channel M-Net has, of course, produced short films in Nigeria, plus several television series through its sister company Africa Magic, but it has never attempted a full-length feature.

South Africa is still far from making a real alliance between the frenetic production of Nigerian videos and its own highly ambitious cinematic tradition, which is more concerned with international recognition than it is with the African market.[11] The first signs of such an unlikely alliance took place, however, in April 2006 during the African Cinema Summit organized in Pretoria, when an agreement between Nigeria and South Africa brought about the re-establishment of the Pan-African Federation of Filmmakers (FEPACI) to the detriment of the largely discredited Francophone representatives who previously dominated the African film industry. Albert Egbe, the Nigerian actor and producer who recently established himself in South Africa, was elected treasurer of the federation, while Madu Chikwendu, a 'big noise' in Nollywood became secretary for the West Africa section. If the Nigerian video industry is to evolve by facing up to the outside world, it will do so through its own expansion beyond its frontiers, and not by the occasional incursion of foreign professionals into Nigeria.

On the global scale, and even within the African continent, the Nollywood phenomenon is completely atypical, just as Nigeria itself is atypical. In the 1990s, at a time when Nigeria had more than ever before drawn back within its own frontiers, cut off from the world and its attentions,[12] there was a shift of some kind that led to the creation of this new mode of production. Nollywood is the beast, venturing out of its lair. Dazzled and bewildered it encounters the outside world with

11. South Africa's film industry is geared towards international recognition at the highest level. In its quest for recognition, the first prize awarded to Zola Maseko's film *Drum* at FESPACO was just the start. Considered much more significant was the Golden Bear awarded in Berlin to *uKarmen eKayelitsha,* and above all the Oscar nominations of *Yesterday* and then *Tsotsi* (the latter won Best Foreign Film in 2006). In line with the industry's strategy, even the internal South African market is of secondary importance. Nollywood, by contrast, has a lasting obsession with its local audience and has a disdain for the international norms which would allow it access to the more 'prestigious' markets.

12. The ferocity of Sani Abacha's regime caused Nigeria to be excluded from the Commonwealth in 1995, and the level of insecurity which continues to this day still discourages many potential visitors.

a mixture of ingenuousness and self-assurance. It hears talk of norms and conformity, and becomes aware of its own non-conformity. But no matter what, its huge energy drives it onwards. Now that it is out in the world it will be difficult to stop and even more to tame.

Films Cited

Abeni (I and II) Tunde Kelani (2005)
Across the Niger Kingsley Ogoro (2004)
Across the River Izu Ojukwu (2004)
Agogo Eewo Tunde Kelani (2002)
'am in Love Andy Chukwu (2007)
Another Great Mistake Mike Bamiloye
Apostle Kasali Amaka Igwe (2004)
Baby Police Uzo Philips
Bai Bureh Goes to War Fred Amata
Black Gold Eddie Ugbomah (2005)
Blood Money
Blood Sisters Tchidi Chikere
Buri Bala Babinlata
Claws of the Lion Francis Onwochei (2005)
Dangerous Twins (I, II and III) Tade Ogidan (2004)
Dangerous Affair
Domitilla Zeb Ejiro (1997)
Die Another Day
Echoes of War Obi Emelonye
Emotional Crack Lancelot Imasuen (2003)
Festival of Fire Chico Ejiro
Gamji John Flash Stephen (2004)
Just a Little Sin Mike Bamiloye
Heritage Ladi Ladebo (2003)
Highway to the Grave Sonia Cacchus
Hit the Street Chico Ejiro (2004)
Hostages Tade Ogidan
Igodo Don Pedro Obaseki
Ileke Greg Odutayo
Issakaba (I to IV) Lancelot Imasuen
Iyawo Alhaji (I and II) Tunde Alabi-Hundeyin (1995, 2001)
Jealous Lovers (I and II) Adim Williams (2003)
Khusufi (I and II) Ali Nuhu (2003)
Late Marriage Adim Williams (2003)
Legal War (2007)
Living in Bondage (I) Chris Obi Rapu (1992)
Living in Bondage (II) Christian Onu (1993)
Ninety Degrees Mak Kusare (2006)
Oduduwa (I and II)

Osuofia in London (I and II) Kingsley Ogoro (2003, 2004)
Peacemaker Chika Onu (2003)
Pretty Woman I. Onyeabor
Raging Storm Tade Ogidan (1998)
Rattlesnake (I and II) Amaka Igwe
Ruhi Hafizu Bello (2002)
Sa'adatu D. A. Baba
Sangaya Auwalu Sabo
Sango Femi Lasode (2000)
Saving Alero Tade Ogidan (2000)
Saworoide Tunde Kelani (2000)
Sayen Baki Mahmud Tijani (2003)
Sharon Stone (I, II and III) Louis Isikaku
Sitanda Izu Ojukwu (2007)
State of Emergency Teco Benson
Suicide Mission Fred Amata
The Addict Fred Amata (2007)
The Apple Lancelot Imasuen (2000)
The Campus Queen Tunde Kelani (2004)
The Game of Life Jeta Amata *(2003)*
The Mourning After Jimi Odumosu (2004)
The Narrow Path Tunde Kelani (2006)
The President Must not Die Zeb Ejiro (2004)
The Story of My Life Mike Bamiloye
Thunderbolt (Magun) Tunde Kelani (2000)
Timi the Village Girl Moses Ebere
Tubali (I and II) Rabiu Ibrahim
Under Fire Tchidi Chikere
Wasila (I, II and III) Yakubu Lere
Widow Kingsley Ogoro (2006)

A selection of Nu Metro films
In 2003, having branched out to Nigeria, the South African company Nu Metro wanted to tap into the experience of Nigerian film distribution. This incursion into the domain of the 'marketers' led to the following section of home-video hits:

The Gardener Patrick Doyle (1997)
Domitilla Zeb Ejiro (1997)
Onome (I and II) Opa Williams (1996)
Violated (I and II) Amaka Igwe (1996)
Mortal Inheritance Zeb Ejiro (1996)
Oorepe Biodun Olaribigbe (2000)
Thunderbolt Tunde Kelani (2000)
Out of Bounds Richard Mofè-Damijo (1997)
Living in Bondage (I) Chris Obi Rapu (1992)
Living in Bondage (II) Christian Onu (1993)

Further Reading

Africa Update Newsletter Vol XI, N°2: 'The Nigerian Film Industry', Central Connecticut State, 2004.

Aihie, Okoh *African Movie Directors in their Own Words*, National Film Institute, Jos, 2004.

Balogun, Françoise *Le cinéma du Nigeria*, L'Harmattan, Collection Cinémédia, Paris, 1984.

Barlet, Olivier. *Les cinémas d'Afrique noire: le regard en questions, Collection Images plurielles*, L'Harmattan, Paris, 1996.

Barrot, Pierre (ed.) *Nollywood: le phénomène video au Nigeria, Collection Images plurielles*, L'Harmattan, Paris, 2005.

Bickford-Smith, Vivian & Richard Mendelsohn *Black and White in Colour: African History on Screen*, Cape Town, Juta/Oxford, James Currey/Athens, Ohio University Press, 2007.

Diawara, Manthia *African Cinema, Politics and Culture*, Indiana University Press, Bloomington, 1992.

Förster, Till & Onookome Okome *Modes of Seeing and the Video Film in Africa*. Köppe Verlag, Cologne, Germany, 2001.

Gugler, Josef *African Film: Re-Imagining a Continent*, Oxford, James Currey/Bloomington, Indiana University Press, 2003.

Haffner, Pierre 'L'Afrique panafricaniste des cinéastes [1960–1985]', *Le film africain*, no. 37–38, 2001: 85–95.

Haynes, Jonathan 'Political critique in Nigerian Video Films', in *African Affairs*, vol. 105, October 2006: 511–33.

Haynes, Jonathan 'Le boum de la vidéo au Nigeria', in *Cinémas africains, une oasis dans le désert?* Ciném'Action n°106, 1er quarter, 2003, Corlet-Télérama, France.

Haynes, Jonathan (ed.), *Nigerian Video Films,* (revised edition), Ohio University Centre for International Studies, 2000.

Haynes, Jonathan (ed), *Nigerian Video Films*, Nigerian Film Corporation, Nigeria, 1997.

Lelievre, Samuel *Les cinémas africains, une oasis dans le désert?* Ciném-Action no. 106, Corlet/Télérama, Paris, 2003.

Maier, Karl *This House has Fallen*, Penguin Books, London, 2001.

Milon, Thomas 'La production audiovisuelle au Nigeria – singularité

Further Reading

et stratégies', in *Le Film Africain et le Film du Sud*, Amiens, May 2001.

Montfort, **Patrice** 'Nigeria: le raz-de-marée de la home video', with interviews with Tunde Kelani and Zeb Ejiro, *Africultures* no. 45, February 2002, L'Harmattan, Paris.

Murphy, David *Sembene: Imagining Alternatives in Film and Fiction*, Oxford, James Currey/Trenton, NJ, Africa World Press, 2000.

Okome, Onookome 'Loud in Lagos: Home Video', *Glendora*, African Quarterly on the arts, vol. 2, no. 1, 1997: 75–83.

Okwori, Jenkeri Zakari 'A dramatised society: representing rituals of human sacrifice as efficacious action in Nigerian home video-movies', *Journal of African Cultural Studies*, vol. 16, no. 1, 2003.

Schmidt, Nancy, J. *Sub-Saharan African Films and Filmmakers, 1987– 1992: An Annotated Bibliography*, London, New Providence (NJ), Hans Zell Publishers, 1994.

Thackway, Melissa, *Africa Shoots Back: Alternative Perspectives in Sub-Saharan Francophone African Film*, Oxford, James Currey/Bloomington, Indiana University Press, 2003.

Nigerian Periodicals
Nollywood
Big Screen
Movie Africa

Further Viewing

Contacts

Le Service de Coopération et d'Action culturelle of the French Embassy in Nigeria has been involved for several years in co-operation with Nigerian producer organizations. Contact: Attaché audiovisuel régional, Consulat général de France à Lagos, 128 bis rue de l'Université, 75 351 Paris SP 07 • www.ambafrance-ng.org

Fespaco Pan-African Film & TV Festival of Ouagadougou • www.fespaco.bf

Pan African Film Festival • www.paff.org

The Open University project on the Nollywood Film Industry and the African Diaspora in the UK. Contact: Dr Françoise Parent Ugochukwu • www.open.ac.uk/Arts/ferguson-centre/nollywood-uk/index.html

Websites selling Nigerian & other African films

nigeriamovies.net (DVD)
africanmoviesdirect.com (V-CD)
allafricanmovies.com (V-CD)
nigeriafilms.com (V-CD)
izognmovies.com (V-CD)
jjjnigermovies.com (V-CD)

Websites of the stars/actors

Jim Iyke jimiyke.net
Ini Edo iniedo.tv
Omotola Ekeinde omotola.tv
Ramsey Nouah ramseysworld.com
Stephanie Okereke stephanieokereke.com
Rita Dominic ritadominic.com
Richard Mofe Damijo rmdpromotions.com
Zack Orji zackorji.net
Ibinabo Fiberesima ibinabofiberesima.com
Clarion Chukwurah clarionchukwurah.com
Kate Henshaw Nuttal katehenshawnuttal.com
Onyeka Onwenu onyekaonwenu.com

Index

Index

Index